LUNCH
TELEPHONE NO. / ROOM NO.
1.00 p.m.
Suite 346
201
540
536
16 1/c
Suite 261

Marc Walter

Voyages
Around the World

Alain Rustenholz
Sabine Arqué

FRIEDMAN/FAIRFAX

Sunlight pierces the foliage as the
curtain lifts on Agra, capital of the
Mogul empire and Moslem dynasty
that once ruled northern India and
whose monarch celebrated the
memory of his favorite wife with a
white marble mausoleum set with
precious stones: the Taj Mahal (p. 2-3).
Of the many palaces that have borne
this famous name, none is so
renowned as the original Taj in Bombay.
One of its old visitors books records
the name of author Somerset
Maugham, secret agent. *East of Suez* –
the title of one of his plays – (p.4).
This celebrated Englishman of French
culture, a man fascinated by
Gauguin's quest for Tahiti, and author
of the words on the label of a Polish
vodka distilled from bison grass,
was truly a traveler.

Design and production:
Marc Walter/Studio Chine
Editorial direction:
Sabine Arqué/Studio Chine
Maps: Florence Cailly,
Hervé Droin/Studio Chine
Translated from the French
by Florence Brutton
Photoengraving: Arte Grafica
Printing: Milanostampa Spa, Italy

Contents

A

"Traveling for me is not arriving: it is departing. It is the flavor of a new day, the unexpected at the next stop, the eternally unfulfilled desire to know more, the curiosity to compare one's dreams with the real world. It is tomorrow, forever tomorrow. As I leave, craning my neck, I would like to be the prow of the ship that is buffeted by the wind and sprayed by the spume." (Roland Dorgelès, *Partir . . . .*) ❦ This is a journey in pictures and words for all those inveterate dreamers, peaceful adventurers and passengers in transit here on earth. One hundred and fifty years of photography, punctuated by quotations from writers and travelers, together bear witness to a world of fleeting, moving, fragile beauty that is increasingly threatened. This is a grand tour across time and continents, an invitation to cast off and set sail for the open seas, following in the footsteps of those "seekers of distant lands" of yesterday and today. ❦ London in the small hours: the city bathes in the gray light of dawn and the Thames is shrouded in yellow fog that renders the river's lighted beacons almost invisible. This is an end-of-the-world morning when it seems the sun will never rise again. Suddenly you feel an irresistible urge to travel afar, on one of those steamships that sail forth from the dock amid the howling of the sirens. It is no accident that the first tourists to yearn for more hospitable shores left from London and other ports in northern Europe. First they headed for the Mediterranean, Italy and Greece, then the East, Egypt, Palestine, India, China, Japan, Australia . . . . ❦ Every account of travel in the 19th century expresses a desire to escape the big city and its sickening smoke in search of warm, colorful climes, fragrant, luminous and serene. Time to pack one's bags and leave. Time for a change of scene and routine. Depart from London, Paris or New York for a few weeks or a few months. Travel to Istanbul, Singapore, Macao or Africa, carried on the waves or steaming cross-country on the *Orient Express* or the *Trans-Siberian Express.* Free to wander, watch the sun set over the ocean or the Atlas Mountains, hear foreign languages, see new faces, follow the caravans to the very limits of the desert . . . . ❦ Those were the happy days of undiscovered lands and immaculate landscapes in all their virgin glory. Those were modern times too, when journeys of discovery might be made in idyllic conditions, both fast and comfortable. Traveling was an adventure because every journey carried an element of the unexpected but without the

risks faced by the explorers of previous centuries. ℰ Yet from 1900 to 1910 there was growing dissatisfaction among the authentic aficionados of the Grand Tour and the eastern route. They complained of running into the Smiths in Cairo or the Rogers in Calcutta when what they wanted was a complete change of scene. It was deplorable to find all these new tourists on the banks of the Nile or at the Acropolis . . . . Witness these few lines from *La Mort de Philae*, Pierre Loti's account of his travels through Egypt in 1907: "Poor Luxor! Along the banks is a row of tourist boats, a sort of two- or three-storied barracks, which nowadays infest the Nile from Cairo to the Cataracts. Their whistlings and the vibration of their dynamos make an intolerable noise." If Loti deliberately painted too black a picture it was because there was nothing in the least democratic about travel at the start of the 20th century – despite the enormous progress made by railways and steamships which did indeed lead to its popularization (in strictly relative terms). Sleeping cars, magnificent liners and grand hotels were there to welcome the rich and titled: diplomats, the wealthy middle-classes, businessmen, writers, fashionable artists, top-ranking government officials and modern-day adventurers seeking to make their fortune. In short, the curious and the carefree, with the means to explore new horizons. ℰ Some of these people – not all of them famous – kept logbooks or captured what they felt on camera. These days we can only gaze longingly at their photographic souvenirs and marvel at the purity and beauty of those unspoiled sites and the naïveté of certain clichés. If "our tourist forefathers" deliberately posed in Arab clothing at the foot of the walls of Jerusalem, or donned turbans outside the Taj Mahal, remember that it was their way of "blending with the landscape" and being accepted. By adopting local clothing, they adopted local customs. There was nothing in the least provocative about it. ℰ Gone is the "golden age" of long-distance travel, the giants of the transatlantic liners, luxury trains and grand hotels. Travelling these days only starts on arrival: the destination is

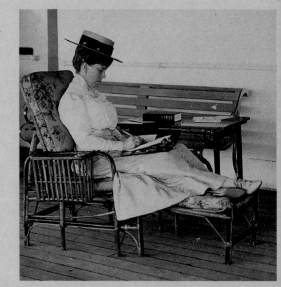

all that matters. In our rush to "get there" we no longer visit the countries on the way, we fly over them. We pass seamlessly from winter to summer, airport to airport and culture to culture, regarding the least delay as a terrible waste of time. Being now weary of running around and traveling ever further and faster in search of false exoticism, travelers in the third millennium try to escape the crowds, the souvenir shops, the "fake" and the standard or commonplace. They long for peaceful walks in unspoiled countryside, a complete change of scene, new contacts and new exchanges: authentic travel! A chance to "leave for the sake of leaving" and travel for the sake of travelling. ❦ They are filled with nostalgia for the magic of transport in "former times": "slow boats" and the soothing purr of train wheels on the tracks. Whatever happened to those infinite horizons and magical shores, steamers with their interminable companionways, the upholstered compartments in sleeping cars and the legendary grand hotels where the atmosphere was both cosmopolitan and gay, serene and familiar? And those shady verandas that looked out to sea, the cool terraces, the twittering of strange birds under the palm trees, the antics of the colorful oropendolas at the Raffles Hotel and the buzzing of insects in the midday heat? ❦ The spirit of travel lives on in all of us. Often we need only stray from the beaten track or deviate from the official route to rediscover the taste of genuine travel. All it takes is an early start or a walk down to the corner of the street. What matters is that we should take a fresh look at everything, want to be astonished, surprised and carried away. That spirit of travel is blowing through these pages.

Sabine Arqué

Above: Air France brochure for the 1938 Douglas DC4 four-engine plane (it began long-haul service only in 1948.
Opposite: Pan-American Airways baggage label (1950s).
Right: 1938 advertising photo of steward and passenger on Paris-London flight.
Previous pages: much-traveled Louis Vuitton woven canvas hat trunk dating from 1896-1914;
Insert: reproduction of a Rome Express train brochure pre-1900 (p.

8); two advertising images for Louis Vuitton: "Smart traveling companions" (1930s, p. 9 above) and "The art of packing" (p. 9 below, 1940s-1950s); Raffles Hotel suite opening onto first floor gallery (p. 10 above); in India, on board the royal yacht Britannia, c. 1890 (p. 10 below); Night falls on the Lake Palace in Udaipur (p. 11).

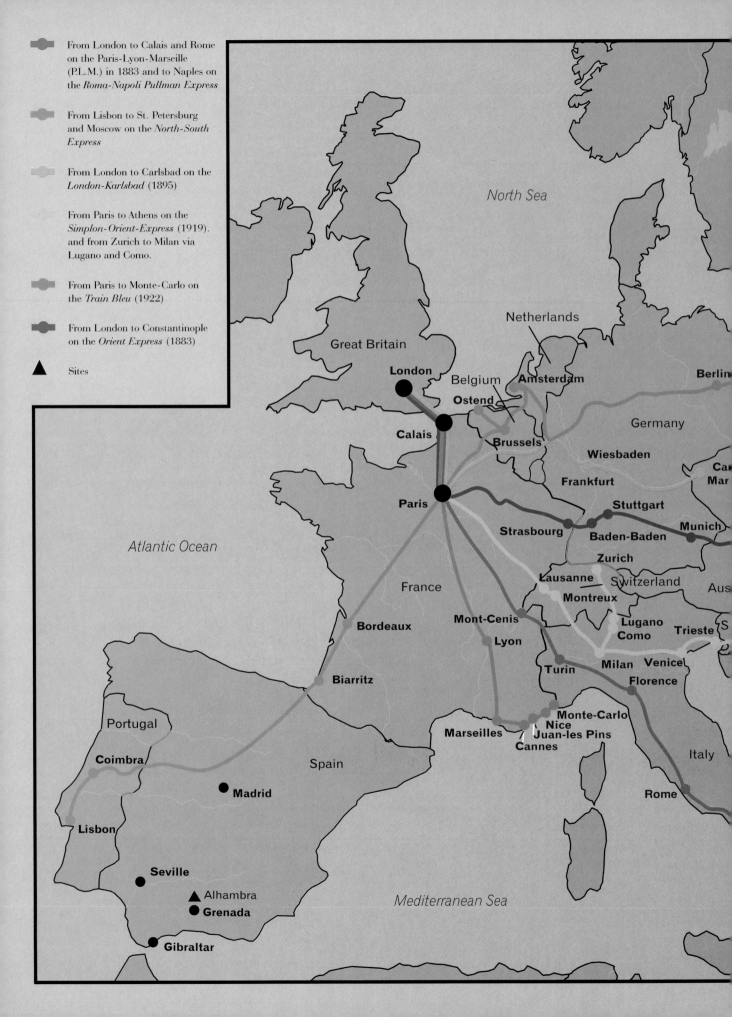

From London to Calais and Rome on the Paris-Lyon-Marseille (P.L.M.) in 1883 and to Naples on the *Roma-Napoli Pullman Express*

From Lisbon to St. Petersburg and Moscow on the *North-South Express*

From London to Carlsbad on the *London-Karlsbad* (1895)

From Paris to Athens on the *Simplon-Orient-Express* (1919). and from Zurich to Milan via Lugano and Como.

From Paris to Monte-Carlo on the *Train Bleu* (1922)

From London to Constantinople on the *Orient Express* (1883)

▲ Sites

North Sea

Netherlands

Belgium

Amsterdam

Berlin

Great Britain

London

Ostend

Germany

Calais

Brussels

Wiesbaden

Frankfurt

Ca
Mar

Stuttgart

Paris

Strasbourg

Baden-Baden

Munich

Atlantic Ocean

Zurich

Lausanne

Switzerland

Aus

France

Montreux

Lugano
Como

Trieste

S

Bordeaux

Mont-Cenis

Milan

Venice

Lyon

Biarritz

Turin

Florence

Portugal

Monte-Carlo
Nice

Coimbra

Marseilles

Juan-les Pins

Italy

Spain

Cannes

Madrid

Rome

Lisbon

Seville

▲ Alhambra

Mediterranean Sea

● Grenada

Gibraltar

European Tour

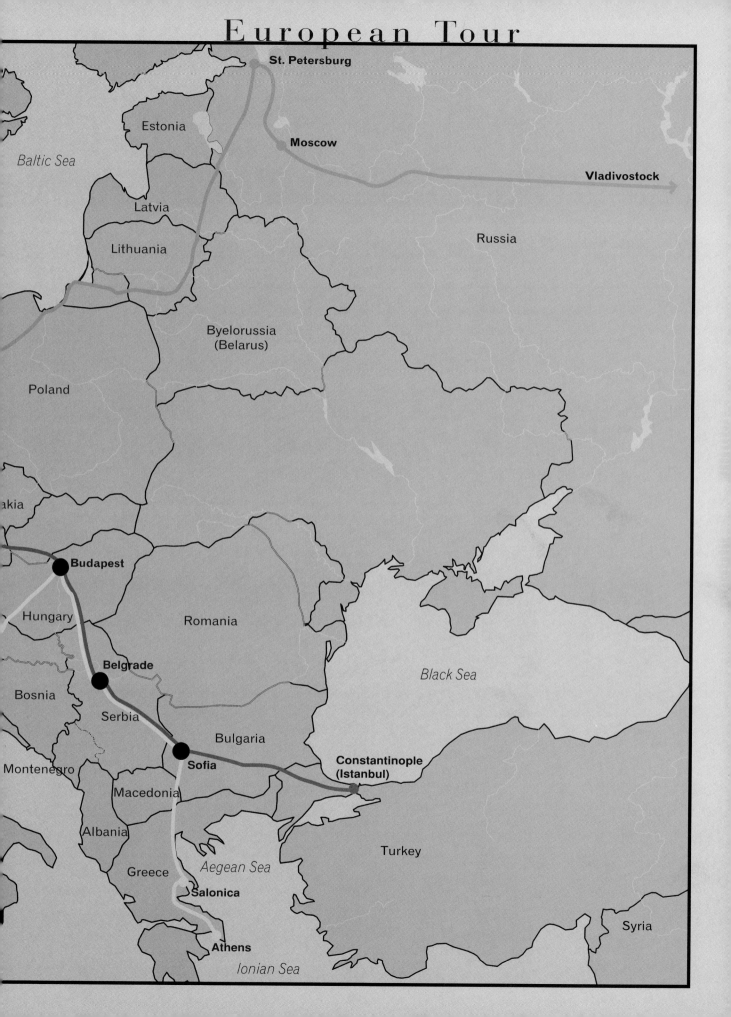

The great trains seethe with impatience at the platforms, plumes of white smoke billowing from their black iron nostrils. Nuggets of greasy coal glisten with the yellow and purple reflections of the furnace. The engine's boiler bubbles and boils ready to pull 1000 feet of Parisian or London "salons" to the opposite end of Europe. A three-day journey to Constantinople, seated at an excellent table, in the smoking room, in a Louis XVth armchair, or maybe perusing the bookshelves in the library. When there is a VIP on board, the staff don French-style uniforms of white pants and stockings. The *Versailles* steams ahead on its steel wheels. The wheel pattern on a Pacific 231 inspired a musical composition by Arthur Honegger. The sheer drive that motivated passengers aboard the *Train Bleu* who "left for the sake of leaving"

inspired a ballet by Darius Milhaud, Cocteau, Chanel and Picasso. ❧ Together these artists span two centuries of history like the two ends of a railway viaduct: the 19th century when Offenbach gave us the "real music of express trains and boats with propellers"; and the 20th century that started with the Futurists. Their canvases "with fast and fleeting, jerky horizontal lines that contrast vividly with the faces in profile and the scrappy strips of leaping countryside, express the turmoil of emotion that is felt by people leaving. ❧ The railways have left their mark on the map of Europe, from London or Paris to Constantinople or St. Petersburg to Lisbon or Madrid-Europe is pitching space against time. Already, for passengers travelling from London to Vienna or Nice to Baden or Ems, Paris is no more than a place where they make their connection. "Book the carriage in advance and make sure it has a good strong horse because I only have 25 minutes to get from the Gare de Lyon to the Gare Saint-Lazare," wrote Offenbach to a friend in 1873. If his opera makes fun of the *Iliad* and the *Odyssey*, the Trojan War and the beautiful Helen, it is because the 19th century saw itself as contemporary and modern; it was time to make a fresh start. ❧ To prove the point, people no longer went to Byzantium to rediscover antiquity, but to Constantinople because it was like going to the ends of the Earth. The English in any case regarded continental Europe as no more than the cross-country portion of the journey covered by the Indian Mail. A boat bound for the Suez Canal would be waiting to meet every train. ❧ Until the Second World War, this was a Europe of Empires and dynasties. One had relations and allies in every country. Trains linked the courts of Carlos I of Portugal, Alfonso XII of Spain and Tsar Alexander III with the Sublime Porte of Sultan Abdül-Hamid. They connected Queen Victoria, the "grandmother of Europe," with her grandchildren, also monarchs: Ludwig II, the mad king of Bavaria, the Emperor Francis-Joseph, Alexander I of Serbia, Ferdinand of Bulgaria and Carol I of Rumania. Next, in the words of A. O. Barnabooth (Valéry Larbaud's picaresque character), came "my

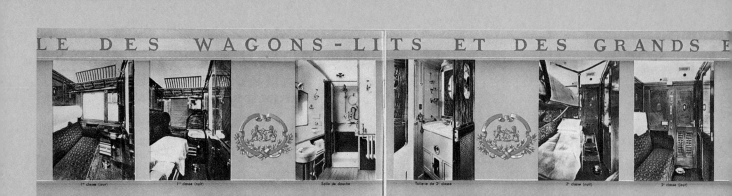

1ʳᵉ classe (jour)   1ʳᵉ classe (nuit)   Salle de douche   Toilette de 2ᵉ classe   2ᵉ classe (nuit)   2ᵉ classe (jour)

Le wagon-restaurant.

COMPOSÉS de voitures-lits de 1ʳᵉ classe (compartiment à une place) et de 2ᵉ classe (compartiment à deux places), d'un wagon-restaurant et de fourgons, le «SIMPLON-ORIENT-EXPRESS» est quotidien, tandis que le «TAURUS-EXPRESS» assure des relations tri-hebdomadaires avec la Syrie, la Palestine, l'Egypte ; bi-hebdomadaires avec l'Iraq, l'Iran ; hebdomadaires avec les Indes.
A Beograd, sont incorporées au S. O. E. les voitures-lits : Ostende-Istanbul, Paris-Est-Istanbul, Paris-Est-Athènes, Berlin-Athènes (tri-hebdomadaire) ; Berlin-Istanbul, Praha-Istanbul (quadrihebdomadaire) ; Vienne-Athènes (hebdomadaire).

I treni «SEMPIONE ORIENTE ESPRESSO» e «TAURUS-ESPRESSO» sono composti di carrozze con letti di 1ᵒ cl. (compartimenti ad un posto) e di 2ᵒ cl. (compartimenti a due posti) di una carrozza ristorante e di bagagli. Il treno S.O.E. è giornaliero; mentre il «Taurus Espresso» assicura tre volte la settimana, le comunicazioni con la Siria, la Palestina, l'Egitto ; due volte la settimana con l'Iraq e l'Iran ; ed una volta la settimana con le Indie.
A Beograd si riallacciano al ramo principale i seguenti servizi di carrozze-letti : Ostenda-Istanbul, Parigi-Est-Istanbul, Parigi-Est-Atene, Berlino-Atene (trisettimanale) ; Berlino-Istanbul, Praga-Istanbul (quadrisettimanale) ; Vienne-Atene (settimanale).

CONSISTING of Sleeping Cars with 1st-class (single-berth) and 2nd-class (double-berth) compartments, restaurant car, and luggage vans, the «SIMPLON-ORIENT-EXPRESS» is a daily service, while the «TAURUS-EXPRESS» provides connection three times weekly with Syria, Palestine and Egypt ; twice weekly with Iraq and Iran ; and weekly with India. At Belgrade, the following services of through sleeping cars link up with the main service: Ostend-Istanbul, Paris-Est-Istanbul, Paris-Est-Athens, Berlin-Athens (three times weekly) ; Berlin-Istanbul, Praha-Istanbul (four times weekly) ; Vienna-Athens (weekly).

DER «SIMPLON-ORIENT-EXPRESS» und der «TAURUS-EXPRESS» bestehen aus Schlafwagen I. Klasse (Abteile mit 1 Bett) und II. Klasse (Abteile mit 2 Betten) sowie Speisewagen und Gepäckwagen. Der «Simplon-Orient-Express» verkehrt täglich. Der «Taurus-Express» stellt folgende Verbindungen her : dreimal wöchentlich nach Syrien, Palästina und Aegypten ; zweimal wöchentlich nach Irak und Iran und wöchentlich nach Indien».
In Beograd werden folgende Schlafwagen mit dem Hauptzüge vereinigt : Ostende-Istanbul, Paris-Est-Istanbul, Paris-Est-Athènes, Berlin-Athènes (dreimal wöchentlich) ; Berlin-Istanbul, Praha-Istanbul (viermal wöchentlich) ; Wien-Athènes (wöchentlich).

peers, those wealthy jet setters from Chicago, Spain and South America, South African magnates, kings, kings of asbestos, kings of oil, the merchant princes" – the extremely wealthy, such as the Brazilian in *Vie Parisienne* or Sir Basil Zaharoff, who supplied the Balkan powder keg with cannons. ℰ This was an open, cosmopolitan Europe; the world was a huge place and space was not an issue. One was at home everywhere and a visiting card was worth more than any passport. A poster for the *Orient Express* in the winter of 1888-1889 makes this abundantly clear: "fast service, no carriage change and,"– in capital letters – "no passport required. Daily departures for Vienna, Wednesdays for Constantinople, Thursdays and Sundays for Bucharest." ℰ From mid-1889, you could travel 2,000 miles from west to east in less than 70 hours – less than three days and three nights. The Compagnie Internationale des Wagons Lits (C.I.W.L.) was like an exclusive club: members were admitted onto the train. There were just 40 passengers on the first *Orient Express* which had two sleeping cars, a restaurant car and a van devoted entirely to luggage. Inside the carriages, the teak panels were lined with Gobelins tapestries, morocco, leather from Cordoba and velvet from Genoa. All the fixtures, from the tables to the blind casings and the inlaid screens, were mahogany. All the fittings, from luggage racks to locks, wall lamps and the lamp bases beneath the silken lampshades, were bronze, French Empire style. Elegance came naturally, even if tuxedos were only required when dining on the St. Petersburg to Cannes train. The art of traveling was part of the art of living. ℰ People went to take the waters in Bohemia on the South Eastern Railway's London-to-Carlsbad service. They went betting at Ascot and Longchamp by "club train" – renamed the "Jockey Club train" by the press. For those who preferred to play on the green baize, there was Monte-Carlo on the Calais-Nice-Rome route or the St.-Petersburg-Vienna-Nice-Cannes route. There were even card tables in the carriages so

passengers could "get their hand in". . . . People took the *Train Bleu* to go bathing on the Côte d'Azur and the Arlberg-Orient-Express to go skiing in winter. There were daily departures in season. ❦ Those who like Edward VII preferred Biarritz to Nice headed for the Côte d'Argent and continued southwards to catch up with the *Andalucia Pullman*, swaying to the rhythm of Ravel and Albeniz all the way to the palace and fortresses of the Moorish kings of

Granada and the Alhambra, with that alabaster basin supported by 12 black marble lions in a courtyard surrounded by 128 white marble columns. ❦ When it reached the end of the line, the rolling palace would rest for a while. The C.I.W.L. parked its palaces in Monte-Carlo and Nice, Opatija on the Croatian Riviera, Lisbon, Constantinople and Ostend and Brindisi, the arrival and departure points for trains connecting with ships to the Indian Ocean. There would be English people there taking the P&O Steam Navigation Company India Mail that cruised Italy once a week connecting with a *Pullman-Express* from Bologna and Brindisi. ❦ Brindisi was "English" in character while Naples on the opposite coast was "French" and remained under Bourbon rule until 1860. So it was that Naples and Versailles were interchangeable as expressions of admiration. On reaching Naples, the continuation of the weekly *Rome-Express* made a stop, but not for long. Soon passengers would be watching through the window as the train pulled away from the platform that "was swept by the billowing skirts of the great express trains."

Alain Rustenholz

Above: Miss Weiss, Viennese actress on the beach of the Grand Hotel des Bains at the Lido in Venice in the 1920s. Opposite: hotel coupons issued to passengers of Thos. Cook's sleeping cars and *Sud-Express* label. Right: fountains and waterfalls at the Caserta Palace near Naples, commissioned by Charles IV, the Neapolitan Bourbon king, in the 1750s and designed by the architect Vanvitelli (picture taken c. 1860-1870).

Previous pages: 1939 advertisement for the P.L.M. Company; Orient-Express poster c. 1890 (p. 17); inner pages of Simplon-Orient-Express brochure (p. 18); *Ricordi di …* souvenirs of Italy: tourist leaflets and postcards – some of panoramic views – dating from 1900-1930, together with a picture of an American lady traveler - and driver – in the 1930s (p. 19).

CAST YOUR EYES OVER London, that city which is forever reinventing itself [. . . .] And then, if you tire of the sight of its people buying and selling, the endless noise of mechanized wheels, the horses, the rolling stock and the locomotives that even in the streets of London pass whistling over your head, then step aside. In the midst of the arid solitude of the crowd, you will find an oasis. On a summer's night in Hyde Park, everything around me was silent except for the birds. There were cows grazing peacefully on the grass [. . . .] An immense horizon stretched away on all sides for as far as the eye could see. I might have been miles and miles from any capital and yet I was in London.

Henri Alphonse Esquiros, 1884

The river Thames which "brings the sea to London" and flows below or past some of the city's principal monuments: London Bridge and the Tower of London of course, but also Westminster, the Houses of Parliament and Big Ben. The Thames, famous for its docks and the Port of London (opposite) which, in centuries past, was one of the largest ports in the world. London, where people only ever went on business, but from where adventurers and travelers departed for the four corners of the world – the Orient, India, America . . . . Right: snapshots of the capital of the British Empire taken by a French visitor in 1891: Whitehall and the Changing of the Guard; the Port of London, and a small French-English dictionary dating from the first half of the 20th century. Following double-page display: Regent Street, the main commercial thoroughfare in London lined with smart boutiques and already very congested.

WHAT ENAMOURED ROD STEIGER WERE THE SHOWER HEADS - nine and three-quarter inch diameter, water cascading straight down from two hundred and ninety holes - and he ordered one. It was more customary for guests to unscrew the heads and steal them; [...] The Savoy bath - six feet long, thirty-one inches wide — poses even greater difficulties for the larcenous, so envious guests are reduced to ordering them.

Israel Shenker, 1988

London's grand hotels: view of the entrance of the Savoy (opposite) and, inset, custom-printed postage stamp for the Hyde Park hotel. Right: Art Deco bedroom at Claridge's. Following double-page display: London welcomes its VIPs with a very kitsch décor straight out of the pages of old Dorchester Hotel brochures. The Oliver Messel suite — named after the decorator — on the 7th floor of the Dorchester, is decorated in the deliberately "modern" style of the 1950s with mirrors on the doors, yellow silk-lined walls and taffeta printed with a rose and oak leaf pattern in the alcove . . . .

THE GORDON HOTELS
LETTERCARD

PRINTED IN ENGLAND

THE GROSVENOR HOTEL

Mrs. Jean Berries
41 Rue Jort...
Pa...

The Savoy Cocktail Book

BEING in the main a complete compen-
dium of the Cocktails, Rickeys, Daisies,
Slings, Shrubs, Smashes, Fizzes, Juleps,
Cobblers, Fixes, and other Drinks,
known and vastly appreciated in this
year of grace 1930, with sundry
notes of amusement and interest concerning them, together with subtle Obser-
vations upon Wines and
their special qualities, and
a complete list of all the most popular an elaborate....

"If all be true that I do think,
There are five reasons why men drink,
Good wine, a friend, or being dry,
Or lest we should be by-and-by,
Or any other reason why."

Aldrich (1647—1710):

The Savoy of London

REFLECTIONS ON THE FIRST
HUNDRED YEARS

ISRAEL SHENKER

Illustrated by Richard Willson

SHE LAUNCHED INTO IT AGAIN — the streets, how they looked, the crooked winding ones, the alleys, the impasses, the charming little places, the great wide avenues, such as those radiating from the Etoile; then the markets, the butcher shops, the bookstalls, the bridges, the bicycle cops, the cafés, the cabarets, the public gardens, the fountains, even the urinals. On and on, like a Cook's tour. All I could do was roll my eyes, shake my head, clap my hands. "If it's only half as good," thought I to myself, "it will be marvellous."

Henry Miller, 1926

Early morning before 1900: a few
hurried pedestrians on the Place
du Petit-Pont at the junction of the
Quai Saint-Michel and the rue du
Petit-Pont. A heavy cart heads
towards the Hôtel-Dieu on the
right-bank, housewives greet each
other on the sidewalk, people
calmly cross the tramlines right
in the middle of the street. No
crosswalk, no traffic lights, no
noise and no smell of gas for the
customers seated at the terrace
of the café "on the corner." The
cathedral of Notre-Dame, imposing
and serene, towers over the River
Seine and the community of
secondhand booksellers.

GO TO THE RITZ AT DINNER-TIME, which starts from 8.30 to 9.00 pm — people do eat very late these days — and see for yourself the glamorous ladies wrapped in precious furs who skip lightly from their automobiles and, tossing their coats to the valet, reveal their exquisite shoulders rippling with diamonds and pearls. Pearls are in fashion as are Argentine ladies. The other day at the Ritz, someone pointed out a charming Argentine lady who was wearing pearls worth millions round her neck.

Arthur Meyer, 1911

Paris, city of light, home of the Place Vendôme, the Rue de la Paix, great jewelers like Boucheron, Cartier and … the Ritz! "From the moment you arrive, things start to happen. A giant in a cap opens the door for you and if necessary holds up a huge red umbrella as you enter the Holy of Holies." (Jean d'Ormesson). This lady arriving at the Ritz in the 1950s (left) – like Hemingway, the Duchess of Windsor, Gene Kelly, Orson Welles and the Aga Khan before her – really does seem to be curtseying to the majestic hotel as she bows her head to step out of the car. Right: the Place Vendôme virtually deserted in the 1940s. The only signs of the glittering life inside the Ritz are the luxury cars parked on the forecourt outside.
Insert: Regina Hotel leaflet c. 1900. Following double-page display: memories of the glorious days of the great Parisian hotels. A Crillon brochure shortly after the hotel opened in 1909, with a view of the "Salon des Batailles" whose tall windows looked out on the Place de la Concorde; a menu from the Majestic hotel – formerly on the Avenue Kléber but gone today – and a Ritz luggage label.

LE SALON DES BATAILLES
(Angle de la place de la Concorde et de l'avenue Gabriel).

DÉJEUNER
Couvert: 4 fr.

HOTEL MAJ
PARIS

Huitres de Belon la douz. 16.—la

Grape fruit au Marasquin 10. Caviar de la Volga 30.
Jambon de Parme 12. Saucisson de Lyon 6. Bouquet 30.
Oeufs froids Jardinière 8. Tomates Moné

Omelette Paysanne 8. Oeufs poêlés aux
Oeufs frits Mexicaine 8.

Moules Mari
Filets de
1/2 L

...binets de toilette, dont les revêtements sont
... verre ou en émail.

... les pièces, sans aucune exception, sont
... éclairées sur la place de la Concorde,
... Boissy-d'Anglas ou sur les deux vastes
...rieures décorées de verdure.

...onstitue un charme unique dans l'Hôtel
...ce sont les terrasses à l'italienne qui
...essus de la colonnade, et sur lesquelles
... une série d'appartements du dernier
...t d'une vue merveilleuse, non seule-
...nonuments de Paris et sur la masse
... Champs-Élysées, mais même sur
...cons, dont l'air pur vient cares-
...brise du Sud-Ouest.

... commun
...rons

HOTEL DE CRILLON

PARIS

LES REPAS SERVIS A L'APPARTEMENT
SERONT AUGMENTÉS
DE 2 FR. PAR PERSONNE ET PAR PLAT

16 FEVRIER 1932.

REGINA

YOU REALLY MUST SEE MODERN-DAY BRUSSELS, from the top of the Boulevard Botanique, on a fine day when the sun is shining on its white houses crowned with a patchwork of bright red roofs. Old Brussels meanwhile is entirely centered on that magnificent Town Hall Square with its golden 16th-century houses that have elaborate, sculpted façades, huge roofs and charming pinnacle turrets on different levels that stand out against the sky. The town hall itself is a work of art. Beneath the vaulted entranceway [. . . . the visitor's attention is drawn to a nail where the architect is said to have hanged himself owing to goodness knows what flaw in his masterpiece.

Jules Clarétie, 1884

BELGIUM

Belgium, that "land of hospitality rich in works of art" was soon welcoming visitors from all over Europe. They traveled by rail to Brussels and Ostend (the *Ostende-Vienne-Express* connected with the *Orient-Express*) and left the train in Antwerp or Ostend itself which had direct links with England – thanks to no fewer than seven steamships that sailed between Ostend and England at the turn of the century. The place to stay in Brussels was the Métropole Hôtel on the Place de Brouckère where the actress Sarah Bernhardt was a frequent guest. Below: Miss Bernhardt's prettily decorated inscription in the hotel guest-book ("the first shall be the last"). Right: a 1895 illustrated guide to Belgium, a "monograph of Brussels" (the King's House, the Place de Brouckère, the Colonne du Congrès) and a postcard of the Métropole Hôtel (1920s). Also, a view of Ostend beach in 1895 with the Continental and Océan Hotels in the foreground and the Osborne Hôtel in the background. Following double-page display: the very Flemish city of Amsterdam, the Dutch sister town of Bruges and Venice, with its sleepy canals, shady embankments and peaceful residents chatting beneath the trees.

Les Derniers seront les premiers!
Sarah Bernhardt
1914

NOTHING CAN EXPRESS what one feels on entering Granada for the first time. To enter through that immense archway of greenery formed by 100-year-old elms is like being transported to an enchanted land. It puts one in mind of the words of an Arab poem that compared them to emerald vaults.

Gustave Doré and Charles Davillier, c. 1880

"Woman with Mantilla": portrait of a woman of Jerez in the 1930s. Wine (Xerès or sherry) and horses (the famous *cartujana* trained at the Royal School of Equestrian Art) are all part of the flamenco décor, a dance that like the Feria del Caballo – where the horses themselves are dancers – and the harvest festival, is a call to snapping fans and arching bodies. Right: La Casa de Pilatos in Seville, an early 16th-century seigniorial palace that is thought to have been inspired by Pontius Pilate's house in Jerusalem. With its delicately carved stucco, possibly some of the finest Azulejo tiles in all of Andalusia and ancient statues at the corners of the terrace, it brings together all the worlds and ages of the Mediterranean.

Above: luggage label from the Ritz Carlton in Barcelona.
Following double-page display: the Alhambra in Granada featuring the Hall of Justice and the Lion Terrace. In the summer of 1933, Jean-Paul Sartre and Simone de Beauvoir made their first-ever journey there. In the company of another couple, they stayed at the Alhambra Hotel for four days but whereas their friends only went out to visit the cathedral, Sartre and de Beauvoir whiled away the hours in the Palace of the Alhambra. They also wandered around town for a day soaking up the local atmosphere.

BEHING THE GARGOYLES, THE PINNACLES AND THE BATTLEMENTS MARKED WITH THE CROSS OF CHRIST lay spacious bedrooms with cool, generous en-suite bathrooms decked out with a multitude of taps, fittings and beveled mirrors consistent with the luxurious expectations of fin-de-siècle values. The furnishings were of pitch pine or copper in accordance with the English good taste that prevailed all the way to the Russian court. Naturally, there was electricity throughout.

Suzanne Chantal, 1972

260 - PORTUGAL - BUSSACO - PALACE HOTEL E JARDINS

The Buçaco Palace Hotel (above) in the mountainous region of La Reira near Coimbra in Portugal is set among the remains of an ancient 17th-century Carmelite convent. The monks originally planted the estate with noble species of exotic plants and, after the death of the last prior in 1856, the Portuguese State administrator did his utmost to continue improving the surrounding forest. The Portuguese Royal Family spent the summer there in 1877 but it was not until the end of the 19th century that the minister of public works persuaded King Carlos to build a palace and modern grand hotel there. Artists in the modern Portuguese style were commissioned to decorate "ceremonial halls as vast as esplanades." In 1910, the "first guests enjoyed the richness of the décor and the comfort of the installations."

Suzanne Chantal, whom we quote above, gives this poetic description of the exceptional world of the Buçaco Palace Hotel: "It was very beautiful at night when the lights went on inside the hotel, like a huge alabaster lamp in the midst of the dark, fragrant forest. The air was a bit chilly despite our shawls. On moonlit nights, we would venture on foot to the gates of Coimbra." Right: a glimpse of the magnificent décor in one of the hotel lounges.

Littoral Méditerranéen

la Croisette

ND

HOTEL

MAJESTIC

HOTEL NEGRESCO

Littoral Méditerranéen

AT THE HOTEL THE GIRL MADE THE RESERVATION IN IDIOMATIC BUT RATHER FLAT FRENCH, like something remembered. When they were installed on the ground floor she walked into the glare of the French windows and out a few steps onto the stone veranda that ran the length of the hotel. [...] Out there the hot light clipped close her shadow and she retreated – it was too bright to see. Fifty yards away the Mediterranean yielded up its pigments, moment by moment, to the brutal sunshine; below the balustrade a faded Buick cooked on the hotel drive.

Scott Fitzgerald, 1934

COTE D'AZUR

In the Belle Époque, the Pier Casino in Nice (above) was one of the finest places in town.
Right: The Winter Garden of the Municipal Casino, Place Masséna, was renovated by Niermans in 1904-1905. A roulette wheel, a hothouse atmosphere and orchids pollinated by spinning balls …
Following double-page display: on the Corniche overlooking Villefranche harbor, two exiled travelers on a one-way ticket gaze out beyond the ships that brought them, to the country they will never see again.

Previous double-page display: light and beauty on the Côte d'Azur in the early 20th century. Photograph album with two views of La Croisette in Cannes and front cover of a leaflet for the Negresco Hotel in Nice (c. 1900).
Top: baggage label from the Hotel Majestic, Cannes.
Right: Reproduction postcard of Russian church in Nice. There were Russian churches in most of the spas and seaside resorts of Europe that were visited by the grand Russian families.

I DID NOT FEEL TIRED ENOUGH TO GO TO BED. So I strolled into the gaming room — not to play but to wander from table to table observing the players who milled around them [. . .], never looking at their faces but only at a certain point of the table where the players placed their hands and at the particular way they moved their hands.

Stefan Zweig, 1927

The terraces of the Monte Carlo Casino in the Belle Epoque (above) and the Casino itself — shown on the left, with its two oriental towers and its bulb-shaped dome-- designed by the architect of the Paris Opera, Charles Garnier, and built in 1878. It was here until the end of the 19th century, that the Prince of Wales rubbed shoulders with Sarah Bernhardt and fortunes were made and lost beneath the chandeliers in the gaming rooms. Then the press attacked the Casino, claiming that 50 players were driven to suicide every month in the Principality alone . . . . In 1907, when betting became legal on the Côte d'Azur, the management of the Monte Carlo Casino pulled out all the stops in the face of mounting competition from new betting establishments in Cannes, Nice, Menton and Juan-les-Pins. The casino opened up to new forms of entertainment including Diaghilev's celebrated Ballets Russes that were performed there between 1911 and 1914. Above: mother-of-pearl and ivory chips manufactured by the firm of Bourgogne and Grasset. Right: croupiers in 1934 under close supervision as they sort chips on a roulette table. Previous double-page display: in September 1938, tourism became more democratic. There were bus trips along the Corniche for a new breed of tourist: men in shirtsleeves, others in T-shirts and berets, and women wearing dresses and flowery hats. The atmosphere on board this open-topped bus is innocently flirtatious.

ROUTE DES ALPES ET DU LITTORAL   S.N.C.

Monaco Monte Carlo
2 Septembre 1938

THE ENTIRE CATHEDRAL RESEMBLES SOME MAGNIFICENT, COLOSSAL CRYSTALLINE CREATION, such is the profusion of pinnacles, the mesh of ribs, the crowd of statues and the intricate lacework of embroidered, hollow, perforated marble that rises up, severally and innumerably, in white outline against the blue sky. [...]. Architecture [...] has lost its sense of purpose: it cares little whether its building is solid or fragile; it does not shelter, it makes a statement [...]. It is born of sublime folly and commits a sublime folly.

Henri Taine, 1864

Cut away until nothing remains but ribs, Milan cathedral bears an uncanny resemblance to the temple in Madura, the stony lacework of the Alhambra or the Shinto temple of Nikko. It is as though across the face of the earth the same filigree of faith symbolized the elevation of the spirit. For those seeking the company of men and "ground level" exchanges, the Victor-Emmanuel Gallery starts at the triumphal arch to the north of the square (on the left of the photo) and leads to La Scala Opera House, passing several bars and boutiques along the way. These, together with the arcades under the Piazza, are the hub of Milanese life. Following double-page display: the waiting-room in Milan's Central Station looks so much like the lounge in a grand hotel that departing passengers may think that they have already arrived and their journey is no longer necessary. A reconstruction project planned in 1906 went ahead in 1912 when architect Ulisse Stacchini was commissioned to rebuild the station. Work was interrupted by the war and only reached completion 20 years later, at the height of fascism. With its ornate 780-foot façade of monumental allegorical statues, the building stood as a glorious showcase for the new regime. The opulent beauty of the interior design bears the stamp of Neo-Classicism and Art Deco. The accent is on space, light and quality of materials. The tone – of luxury and serenity – is established by the grandiose and refined waiting room.

AT THE TOP OF THE SCENTED HILLSIDE, among the cypress trees and statues – visitor, rub your eyes! There at your feet is the Ponte Vecchio, the cathedral, the campanile, the Old Palace and Florence, asleep in the dust of centuries.

Gaston Leroux, 1925

the Medusa. At the back of the square, partly hidden by the large pillar, stands the solid square outline of the Orsanmichele, a former grain warehouse converted to a church.

Inset: an entrance ticket to an Italian museum issued by the Minister of Public Education in 1960.

Previous double-page display: view of the town from San Miniato al Monte on the other side of the Arno. From left to right: the Palazzo di Signoria with its tower, then the Baptistery and the Campanile begun by Giotto and then the cathedral of St. Maria of the Flowers (the Duomo), whose dome Brunelleschi built. In the foreground of the Duomo is the spire of the Badia Fiorentina church (where Dante discovered his Beatrice) and the Bargello tower. Visible above the trees is the church of Santa Croce where Michelangelo is buried.

All the power of Florence, as symbolized by Hercules' muscular back, is expressed in this view of the Piazza della Signoria, c. 1880 (above). On the left and also shown in the picture on the right is the Loggia dei Lanzi: the barracks of the landsknechts (foot soldiers) of the guard, set with aggressive Roman or Renaissance statues such as Benvenuto Cellini's Perseus brandishing the head of

"We were staying in a hotel on Pantheon Square that according to our guidebook was the cheapest in town: the Albergo del Sole where Cervantes once lived." The "we" refers to Jean-Paul Sartre and Simone de Beauvoir and the date is 1933 (the photograph above was taken 50 years earlier). Two years later, they "spent 10 days at the Albergo del Sole and ate porchetta on Pantheon Square." The hotel was built in 1467 and some of its bedrooms had magnificent painted ceilings. These days the Albergo del Sole is a five-star hotel and one of the most expensive in Rome. The couple always remained faithful to it.

Right: The Trevi Fountain with its back to the palace of the Dukes of Poli. Oceanus, on a carriage in the shape of a conch drawn by two marine horses and led by Tritons, brings the roar of the waterfall to the heart of the town.
Following double-page display: the Roman Forum. From left to right: the three evocative Corinthian columns that since the 6th century A.D. have supported the marble entablature of the temple of Castor and Pollux; the foundations of the columns of the Basilica Julia, built by Julius Caesar, the largest basilica in the forum, and dedicated to the discussion of civil affairs; the elegant gray and pink

granite portico of the Ionic temple of Saturn, built in the 4th century A.D.; the Phocaean Column, topped with fluted white marble and built in 608 A.D. by Pope Boniface IV in honor of the Byzantine Emperor Phocas - in return for his gift of the Pantheon, henceforth a church dedicated to the Virgin and all the Martyrs; the arch erected by Septimius Severus and his two sons in 200 A.D. following a victory against the Arabs and the Parthians of Mesopotamia.
Insert: reproduction of brochure for the Quirinal Grand Hotel, c. 1900.

TOLEDO STREET BELONGS TO EVERYONE. It belongs to the restaurants, the cafés and the shops; it is the thoroughfare that supplies and crosses all of the districts in town [...]. The nobility drive there, the middle-classes sell their fabrics there and the working-classes take a nap there. An excursion for the nobles; a bazaar for the merchants; home for the *lazzarone* [...]. Next to the traditional hostelry with its fly-blown curtains, an elegant pastry cook displays his wife, his brioches and his rum babas. Opposite a respectable manufacturer of antiques destined for Messrs the English struts a person selling chemical matches. Finally [...] there is Toledo street, paved with lava like Herculanum and Pompei and lit by gaslight like London and Paris.

Alexandre Dumas père, 1835

Toledo Street is the continuation of the Via Roma (above, c. 1910). Let us see what Sartre and de Beauvoir had to say about it in 1935: "We used to buy our dinner on the street, sandwiches or cold chicken, which we ate on the hoof [...]. The words "inside" and "outdoors" had lost all meaning. The gloomy caves with their softly glowing icons belonged to the street; sick people lay asleep on the grand marriage bed, dead people lay resting uncovered. And the intimacy of the houses pervaded the entire street. Tailors, shoemakers, blacksmiths, people making artificial flowers and craftsmen worked in their shop doorways; women sat on their front steps delousing their children, washing linen and gutting fish, meanwhile keeping an eye on the basins of crushed tomatoes that they had set out under the distant blue sky. Smiles, looks and friendly voices flowed from one end of the street to another. We were touched by such kindness. [...] Escaping the hardships of Naples, we discovered that it had a softness about it."

Right: the Gradoni di Chiaia, c. 1900, a street made of steps. Following double-page display: those glorious days at the end of 19th century when there were three guides for every two tourists! These two seem to be asking their way as ordinary passers-by might ask a policeman ... And so it is that at the foot of "its" Vesuvius, Pompei still seems to be alive.

THUS IT WAS that he saw it once more, that most astonishing of all landing-places, that dazzling composition of fantastic architecture which the Republic presented to the admiring gaze of approaching seafarers: the unburdened splendour of the Ducal Palace, the Bridge of Sighs, the lion and the saint on their two columns at the water's edge, the magnificently projecting side wing of the fabulous basilica, the vista beyond it of the gate tower and the Giant's Clock; and as he contemplated it all he reflected that to arrive in Venice by land, at the station, was like entering a palace by a back door; that only as he was now doing, only by ship, over the high sea, should one come to this most extraordinary of cities.

Thomas Mann, 1913

"And there was Venice. Leaving the station, I was amazed to see tourists telling the gondoliers to take them to their hotels; they were going to settle in, open their cases, get cleaned up. I hoped I would never become that sensible. We left our cases with left luggage and walked for hours; our sight of Venice was a sight that we shall never experience again: the first sight." (Simone de Beauvoir)
The sight we see here could be a lady tightrope walker preparing to climb onto her wire and using her parasol as a pole (Saint Mark's Square, c. 1880).
Inset: luggage label from Bauer Grünwald Hotel.

Following double-page display: "Who can paint that vague, luminous atmosphere full of rays and vapors, where sunshine does not exclude clouds? That coming-and-going of gondolas, boats [...] ..." Thus pondered Théophile Gautier in 1850. Today more than ever we need to interpret Venice if we wish to express its soul.
To our eyes, gondolas at rest on the deserted lagoon opposite San Giorgio represent a timeless, poetic vision of Venice.

THE SHOUTS OF THE GONDOLIERS WERE THE SAME AS THEY HAD BEEN 40 YEARS EARLIER: so too was their skill in avoiding the other gondoliers at the corners of the waterways. [...] They took a few steps along the embankment and saw the *Marco-Polo* floating on the lagoon. The ship had just arrived: tomorrow it would take Christine away [...]. His gaze went stupidly from the water to Christine to the ship. That was how the good life ended, with a ship, a cabin and a woman going away. Leaning against the rail, facing St Mark's Square, Christine watched as an old man surrounded by strangers pulled away in a launch.

Edouard Lavergne, 1941

Vaporetti (c. 1910, left). The changing noise of the propellers, boats going astern and going ahead, zigzagging across the water to moor up either side of the Grand Canal - the sounds of a major port brought to the heart of the city.
Right: the steps leading up to the Rialto Bridge – a place that is usually teeming with tourists – seem more packed with locals in this picture.
Following double-page display: outside the cabins of the Excelsior Hotel at the Lido (in 1905), the Rumanian Royal Family whiles away the hours looking at photographs of the city taken a few days earlier . . . .
Insert: 1950s leaflet for the Bauer Grünwald Hotel.

Lᴀᴋᴇ Cᴏᴍᴏ, ѕᴏ ᴇᴀѕʏ, ѕᴜᴄʜ ᴀɴ ɪɴᴅᴜʟɢᴇɴᴛ ᴄʟɪᴍᴀᴛᴇ, always sending visitors off on one of those boats where they can stretch out and daydream; the ideal place for people with no desire to resist their passion. That lightness of air, so elegant as to be bland, was for centuries but the fragrant breath of youth and pleasure. Occasionally, on one of those fine days that were so slow, so lazy and so blue, one would wish for the lake to swell slightly. I never found it noisier than the rustling of silk on a woman's skin.

Maurice Barrès, 1893

"What is there to say about Lake Maggiore, the Borromean Islands or Lake Como except to express sympathy for any person who does not love them to distraction?" wrote Stendhal, adding that Bellagio was "[his] pearl, rivaled but not surpassed by the Bay of Naples." Right: former brochures for the Villa Serbelloni Grand Hotel,

"a first-class hotel of international repute with 220 beds, 80 private baths, good orchestra, open-air dancing, large grounds and gardens." Magnolias, pomegranate trees, oleanders and olive trees add their fragrance to colors that seem fixed fast in the steely blueness of Lake Como.
Insert: 1930s leaflet showing the Villa Serbelloni with views over Lake Como.

GOING INTO MONTREUX Dick pedalled slowly, gaping at the Dent du Jaman whenever possible, and blinded by glimpses of the lake through the alleys of the shore hotels.

Scott Fitzgerald, 1946

Passing through Switzerland, one could see the sailboats on Lake Geneva (above) and the colorful façades of the houses in Berne (right).
"The historical perseverance of that city [...], that city dweller's frame of mind which is still so much in evidence there [...]. It is occasionally worth remembering that in their youth those same middle-class folk erected monuments of solemn unity and knew how to stamp their sober, resolute and piously unshakeable character on the entire town." (Rainer Maria Rilke, letter to Merline, 4 August 1919).
Inset: Hotel du Parc baggage label.

Previous double-page display: Steam ship in Ouchy, in front of the Beau-Rivage Grand Hotel on the lake. "Love in Ouchy this weekend together at the Beau-Rivage Hotel you see I am my aunt's niece I was not accustomed to such luxury hotels you remember that's the life for me I said gloriously pacing up and down it's true to live forever with him in a hotel and never see another soul would be wonderful [...] oh! that night in Ouchy in the bed where I waited for him while he was bathing [...] come my Sol and live with me at the Beau-Rivage," Ariane's monologue in *Belle du Seigneur* by Albert Cohen.

LAUSANNE-OUCHY

HÔTEL DU PARC

AT SPAS [...], hotel landlords and managers are guided in their allotment of rooms to visitors, not so much by the wishes and requirements of those visitors, as by their personal estimate of the same. It may also be said that [they] seldom make a mistake. [...] What everyone took the Grandmother to be I do not know [...]; without delay they entered her in the hotel register as "Madame la Générale, Princesse de Tarassevitcheva", although she had never been a princess in her life. Her retinue, her trunks, portmanteaux, and strong-boxes, all helped to increase her prestige.

Dostoevsky, 1866

Wittgenstein and Chancellor Gorchakov - passed by in their carriages. Another friendly trio, Ivan Turgenev with the singer Pauline Viardot and her husband, was close at hand in the lounges of the House of Conversation (top left) or at the French Jockey Club races held at the Iffenzheim track (below). In the summer of 1865, Gustave Flaubert came to visit. At the end of November, the spa closed down completely and everybody returned to town. Right: Wiesbaden (c. 1910), another famous spa and gaming town and also the setting for *The Gambler* by Dostoevsky. This brochure for the Schwarzenbock Hotel sings the praises of "one of the most beautiful German spa towns of the Taunus and the Rhineland." Note however that what this famous establishment is promoting (on the front of the leaflet, what is more) is the casino. Seen in the background is a photo of the Kochbrunnen Spa taken from a late 19th century illustrated guidebook.
Following double-page display: the crystal chandeliers in the Florentine room of the casino in Baden-Baden.

Europe had two capitals: Paris in winter and Baden-Baden in summer. In early July, the *ménage à trois* made up of Maxime du Camp and the Hussons settled in Alleehaus, the villa located directly opposite the Lichtentaler Allee where the nobility - the Grand Duke of Baden, the Count of Pourtalès, the Prince of

Wiesbaden

das schönste deutsche Heilbad
am Taunus und Rhein.

HOTEL EUROPE HEIDELBERG

Berlin in 1920 – "Athens on the Spree" to the erudite and "Chicago on the Spree" to energetic capitalists - was a town undergoing major change that ranked as the second most important city in Europe. It still had its Versailles: Potsdam, home of the royal palaces, the elegant residential area of Charlottenburg and the slightly more humble suburb of Pankow. The Crown Prince's palace meanwhile, extended all the way from the Unter den Linden to the Behrenstrasse where great banks stood side by side with stately homes. Wilhelm II planted a second tree-lined avenue, the Sieges Allee (the "Heroes Promenade") but "at the crossroads of the Joachimsthaler Strasse and the Kurfürstendamm, Hell has its headquarters. Messel rushed to build this café before he died and Cassirer decorated all the walls with devilish works by Klimt. The floors are covered with mosaics presenting detailed anatomical studies by Hodler.

There, long-haired men with snakelike curls, carelessly knotted ties, Sezession-style socks and bouffant pants, by their vile and decadent habit of coffee drinking take German art to the very edge of the precipice." (extract from an article in *Der Sturm* magazine, Berlin, 1911).

The group photograph above of a tourist bus about to leave was taken outside No. 47 Unter den Linden. Mr Hampel, the photographer to whom we owe this 1930s cliché, would quickly print his photographs then send a cyclist to peddle alongside the moving vehicle and sell them to the passengers.

Inset: baggage label from the Hotel Europe in Heidelberg.

Following double-page display: view from the roofs of Nuremberg in 1895, showing the city's magnificent medieval houses perforated with countless windows. In the 16th century, Albert Dürer's hometown on the banks of the river Pegnitz–a tributary of the Main–was one of the most important artistic centers in Europe for wood engraving, glass painting and enameling, metal and wrought ironwork, porcelain firing . . . . At the time more than 600 master goldsmiths worked in Nuremberg. The city's guilds are featured in *Die Meistersinger von Nürnberg* by Wagner in which the hero, Hans Sachs, a shoemaker by trade, is supposed to have written 6,000 melodies and poems.

I WENT OUT INTO THE STREETS OF THE CITY, into the Berlin of the period, a city so surprised at its own growth […] that every street and every stone was alive with electricity and everyone was filled with an irresistible pulsating rhythm […]. One day, when it drew me to follow a pretty girl, I reached the Unter den Linden and all of a sudden as I stood outside the University I could not help but laugh to think of how long it had been since I had last crossed its venerable threshold.

Stefan Zweig, 1929

I ENDED UP AT THE SACHER HOTEL, the only one I knew. Madame Sacher's establishment had welcomed, with all the spying and discretion required, every prince and marshal in Europe, every Spanish grandee, every Turkish pasha, Russian Highness and Roman cardinal. Years ago when grandmother was staying with her sons, it was Madame Sacher who had taught her the recipe for Sacher Torte, that chocolate cake stuffed with red currants that our cooks still religiously baked for every one of our birthday meals.

Louise Weiss, 1919-1934

which is underground at this point – flowed above ground and under the bridge of St. Elisabeth. The view from the church looked over the "glacis," that huge stretch of land that separated the center of Vienna from its suburbs. Right: typically Viennese atmosphere in one of those literary cafés for which the Austrian capital is so famous. Schnitzler, Altenberg – a model of whom can still be seen reading his newspaper at a table in the Café Central – Hofmannsthal and Brahms were all habitués of the cafés. This sideboard in the Fischbauer Café displays a portrait of "Sissi." Following double-page display: the gazebo in the Schönbrunn Gardens in 1907 - always open to the public even when the Emperor was in residence. Not only did it have a raised gazebo but visitors could also climb up to the gallery … To think of the sights one might have seen through the windows of the Hall of Ceremonies, directly opposite in the castle.

Above: Vienna, St. Charles Square and the gazebo c. 1895. The large cemetery that used to occupy the site in Roman times had long since vanished by the early 19th century when Schubert lived in the house that can be seen on the left of the church of St. Charles Borromeo. Built between 1716 and 1737, it is Vienna's finest baroque church, with a grand portico that is flanked by elegant columns carved with bas-reliefs representing scenes from the life of the saint. When this photograph was taken, the Vienna canal –

In the summer of 1900 when they went to Russia for the second time, Lou Andreas-Salomé left Rainer Maria Rilke in St. Petersburg to visit her parents for a few days. "What I also liked" he mused as he awaited her return, "was the moonlit night between Wednesday and Thursday. It was quite late when I reached my favorite place on the banks of the Neva opposite the Cathedral of Saint Isaac where you can see the city in all its simplicity and in all its grandeur at the same time . . . ."

Above: the four adjoining palaces of the Hermitage Museum on the banks of the Neva – including the Winter Palace – and the Palace Bridge that in this picture hides the foot of the columns. There was no bridge in the days of Peter the Great, a sailor for whom the only way to cross the water was by boat. The strict alignment of the buildings, their uniform height and the absence of gaps between them are reinforced by their perfectly symmetrical reflection in the water that nothing was allowed to disturb. Dostoevsky wrote that this was the "most premeditated" city in the world.

THE STEAMBOAT SET OFF ONCE AGAIN and, standing on the bridge, we looked avidly at the extraordinary spectacle that was unfolding before our eyes. We were in the sound where the Neva pours into the sea. It looked more like a lake than a gulf. As we sailed down the middle of the channel, the banks on either side were barely visible. The wide expanses of water seemed higher than the land, as slim as a brushstroke on a watercolor painted in flat colors. It was a beautiful day. The light from the clear sky was sparkling but cold; it was a boreal sky--polar, one might say--with milky, opalescent, steely nuances that our own skies never begin to suggest; a pure, white, sidereal clarity that did not seem to come from the sun; the kind of light we imagine when transported to another planet in our dreams.

Théophile Gautier, 1866

IN THE LONG STRETCH OF LANDSCAPE THAT SEPARATES ST. PETERSBURG FROM MOSCOW [...] nothing can prepare the eyes for the dazzling spectacle that awaits or the spirit for the surprise that lies in store. [...] On the horizon and off into infinity are masses of domes growing rounder, towers growing taller and square shapes with pointed roofs painted in vivid colors. It is as if a gust of wind had chased away all the mists, a curtain tearing to reveal the Orient. [...] And while your eyelids are still fluttering with this enchanting sight, it is as if you were rocked by a buzzing of bees, like a drumming on copper that throbs in all directions, the multitudinous voice of bells sounding forth from all of these Christian mosques.

Armand Silvestre, 1892

Above: painted photograph of St. Petersburg, c. 1900
Right: the Palace Square with its golden angel resembling Alexander I: cross in hand, he tramples on a serpent that symbolizes Napoleon's invading army. In particular however, the golden angel seems to separate the rigorously classical style of the yellow and white building, home to the General Staff and Foreign Affairs, and the exuberantly baroque style of the blue-green Winter Palace. Next to it stands the New Hermitage that in the mid-19th century prefigured the world-famous museum.

Following double-page display: Red Square, Moscow, c. 1900. On the left, the multi-colored domes of the Cathedral of St. Basil: one with ochre, red and green squares; another with orange, white and green stripes; a third with saffron and green-colored spirals . . . . In the center, the monument to Minin and Pozharsky, two Russian patriots who defeated the Poles; on the right, the walls of the Kremlin. Let us follow Rilke as he heads there on his way to the New Moscow Inn: "Crossing Red Square, past the Cathedral of St. Basil on your left, you take the road straight ahead that crosses the bridge. It is the first large new building on the corner on the opposite bank." Rilke and Lou stay in a round bedroom that she describes as follows: "The loveliest and the most typical rotunda in the inn, with its three windows that give you a view over the whole town and the Kremlin just the other side of a slim window pane."

THINGS ARE MORE AGREEABLE HERE IN MARIENBAD where people are not puffed up with pride just to be here, as they are in Carlsbad. In the large, pleasant grounds the tall, elegant houses that are all hotels are surrounded on all sides by gentle hills that seem to rejoice in the wide pathways leading towards them and forests that are overjoyed to see such nice obese people wandering around. There are smiles too from the waiters, the servants and the porters; whereas in Carlsbad they are all very solemn and take themselves extremely seriously.

Arthur Schnitzler, 1895

MARIENBAD

The late 19th century "new" baths in Marienbad (left) and the neo-baroque Colonnade (above), a long cloister designed for socializing. Its arcades and cast-iron vaulting were like the overhead reflections of the necklaces and pearls that paraded beneath on the polished tiles. One might occasionally see royalty there, one or two actresses, the governor of a bank, a theater manager, and, according to Arthur Schnitzler, "knights of industry, diabetics, Polish Jews, gigolos, a few really elegant people and two or three ravishingly beautiful American women."

Following double-page display: a section of the 72 columns of the Kreuzbrunnen, the source of the Croix, the most important spa in Marienbad. The town was officially declared a spa in 1818 when this pavilion was built. Goethe, Gogol, Kafka and Wagner – who was said to be dreaming of a second Bayreuth – might all be seen wandering the space between its pediment and the bandstand where concerts were performed at dawn.

THIS MORNING UNDER CLEAR SKIES I WALKED UP TO THE ACROPOLIS, climbing the steps of the Propylaea, which used to be a Sacred Way. The columns of the portico, now stripped of their pediment, stand out against the sky between the small Ionic temple of the Apteral Victory and the building opposite. These blue doorways framed by white pillars in the Doric style, doorways made of air and sky that these days lead to the Parthenon, are possibly as majestic if not more so than the bronze doors that originally graced this building. On reaching the top, one wanders among the ruins. [...] On the right, the Parthenon, roofless and without its pediment, beautiful only for its columns and architraves, towers into the sky in all its sun-kissed whiteness, like a golden archway that was once inhabited by a divine thought.

Edouard Schuré, 1889

"Time and the boat slipped softly towards the canal of Corinth. All the way to Piraeus. A taxi took us to Athens along a road full of potholes. [...] We spent the day exploring the streets, the markets and the port, on Mt. Lycabette, in the museums but especially at the Acropolis and on the Pnyx, from where we looked at the Acropolis. Beauty is even harder to describe than happiness. If I say: "I saw the Acropolis; I saw the korai at the Museum," then there is nothing more to say, short of writing another book." (S. de Beauvoir, July 1937). Left, the Port of Piraeus and, right, the Acropolis seen from the northwest, from the Theseium, with the temple of Theseus in the foreground. From left to right on the Acropolis itself, the Erechtheum, ancient temple of Athena, and the Parthenon. Following double-page display: the temple of Zeus Olympian, east of the Acropolis.

THIS VIEW, WHEN SUFFUSED WITH GOLD BY THE SUN that transforms the meanest hovel into a palace, is always magnificent; but there is a time when it seems more marvelous still, on one of those warm eastern nights as your caïque glides silently between the two silent banks. There, dimly visible in the shadows, is that great mute city with its eternally sealed houses that confine so many unknown destinies, so many mysterious lives [...].

Alexis de Valon, 1845

I S T A N B U L

The imperial palace of
Dolmabahçe on the Bosporus
(photo by J. P. Sebah & Joaillier, c.
1880) built entirely of marble and
stucco. In the summer, the Sultan
left for his residences on the
eastern bank where other
privileged people also had their
yali: a palatial villa on the water,
shaded by the hills and fanned by
cooling breezes from the Black
Sea. From there, the wealthy would
set off by caïque for a picnic on
the Princes' Islands.
Insert: baggage label of the Pera
Palas Hotel.

ISTANBUL
PERA PALACE
HOTEL

I LONG TO BE THERE; a force of attraction, an indescribable remembered emotion makes me hurry faster through the night on the endless bridge that leads across an arm of the sea to that city so dark. As I draw closer, the fiery crowns of the domes and the minarets rise higher and higher into the sky. Now I stand at their feet. Leaving the moving floor of the bridge, I step onto the pebbles and potholes of the first dark square that is dominated by the magnificent shape of a mosque – I am in Stamboul.

Pierre Loti, 1890

The Galata Bridge (right) above the Golden Horn links Stamboul (opposite) at one end - the Turkish city that is home Topkapi Palace, the Seraglio, the Divan, the Sublime Porte and Hagia Sophia, visible on the left – with the New Mosque at the other end. On this side is the Christian section of Galata-Pera with its Greek and Armenian churches, embassies, banks, Lycée Français and daily newspapers published in French. Also the Pera Palas, the famous hotel terminus of the Orient Express to Constantinople, built by the Compagnie des Wagons-Lits in 1892.

Left: the central lounge of the Pera Palas c. 1895. Famous guests included Kemal Atatürk, the Begum and members of all the royal dynasties as well as the English spy "Cicero," Mata Hari, and writers and artists of international repute. Agatha Christie, another faithful guest, wrote Murder on the Orient Express at the Pera Palace where she stayed for research purposes from 1926 to 1932 en route from London or returning from Egypt or Mesopotamia.

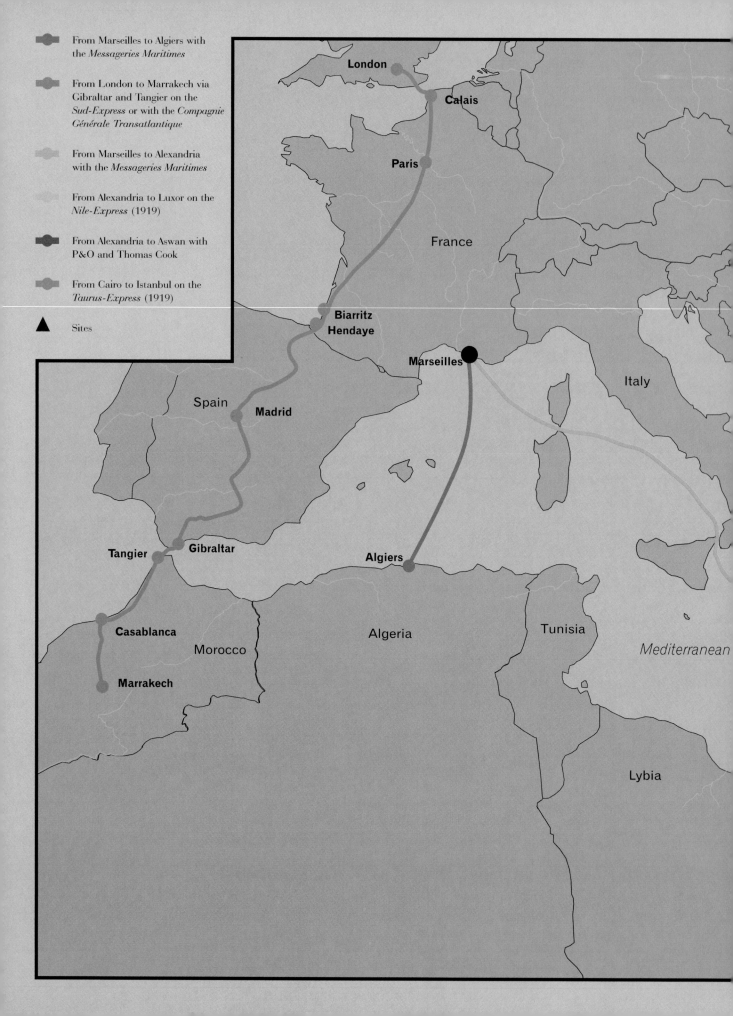

London

Calais

Paris

France

Biarritz
Hendaye

Marseilles

Italy

Spain

Madrid

Tangier   Gibraltar

Algiers

Casablanca

Morocco

Algeria

Tunisia

Mediterranean

Marrakech

Lybia

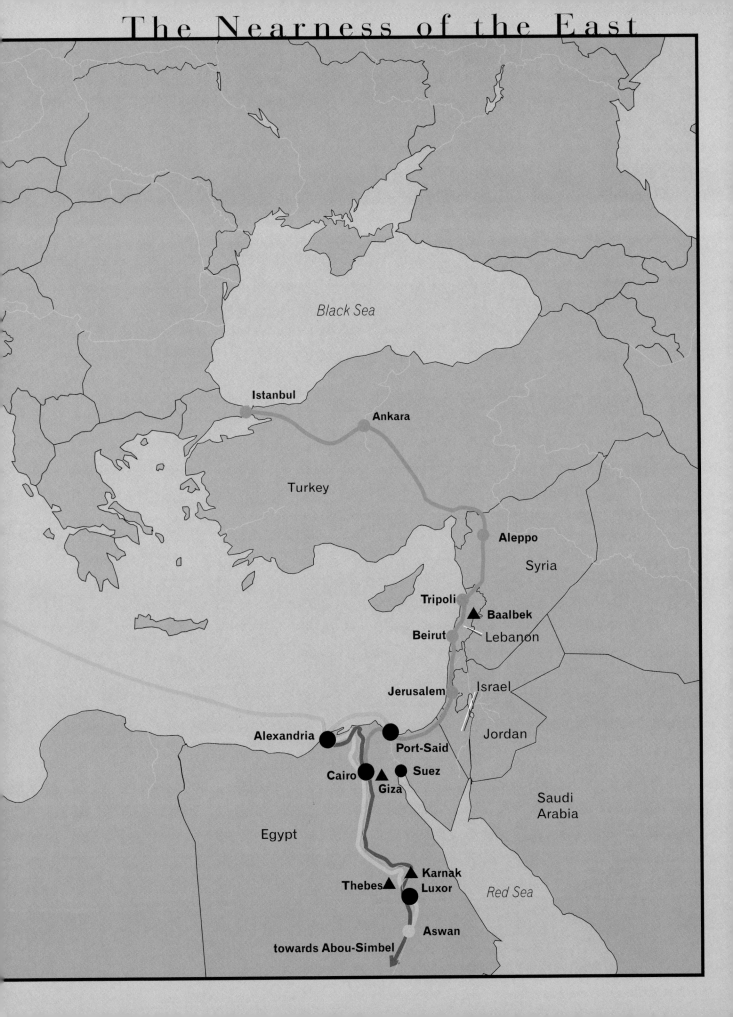

Black Sea

Istanbul

Ankara

Turkey

Aleppo

Syria

Tripoli

▲ Baalbek

Beirut

Lebanon

Jerusalem

Israel

Jordan

Alexandria

Port-Said

Cairo ▲

Suez

Giza

Saudi
Arabia

Egypt

Karnak

Thebes ▲

Luxor

Red Sea

Aswan

towards Abou-Simbel

Port Said.
Le Port

Marseilles, with its flagrant opium dens and rampant prostitution, was the doorway to the East, the Near East and the Far East, a land so exotic that it seemed to grow more remote the closer one approached. In 1925, the *Champollion*, owned by the *Messageries Maritimes*, left for Alexandria and Beirut with 188 first-class passengers on board. The décor was in the modern style as was to be expected in 1924, a year that saw the opening of the Decorative Arts Exhibition. There was no trace of vulgar steel, riveted metal or other construction materials in the wood-paneled and tapestry-lined walls or in the bedroom ceilings. The only iron in evidence was the wrought ironwork on the elevator that was decorated with papyrus and swastika motifs. The same design was inlaid into the wooden niches where Egyptian statues stood guard. ☙ In less than five days the ship would be in Alexandria, the most cosmopolitan city of the Mediterranean, bustling with passengers from Marseilles and ports on the opposite coast: from Istanbul with Khedive Shipping, Trieste with the Austrian Lloyd Line and Brindisi with P & O Shipping. Alexandria was also the end of the line for the *Wagons-Lits*. It was a man from Marseilles, the younger of the Borelli brothers, who started a daily newspaper called *La Réforme* in which he published the travel diary of the poet Rimbaud whom he met in Ethiopia. ☙ On reaching Alexandria, Cairo beckoned and passengers set off with the C.I.W.L. to cover the 550 miles of track along the Nile Valley, valley of kings, queens, nobles and their tombs. The temperature in the carriages of the *Etoile d'Egypte* was maintained at 75°F thanks to a false ceiling where the air was cooled by blocks of ice. Blinds on the windows shaded the light that fell on the leather and mirrors. They also obscured the view, but the banks of the Nile held little interest for most of the passengers who were simply going to winter in the sun at Aswan. Some had already spent long periods at the celebrated Mena House in the shadow of the Pyramids, departing every evening on horseback for shadows that grew more mysterious still only to return to the terrace no wiser and resume their silent contemplation. ☙ On the western bank of the Nile, the railway passed close by the Sphinx and the pyramids of Giza, the ruins of Memphis and the Stepped Pyramid of the Necropolis of Saqqarah. Further south, the date palms and sugar canes of the great oasis of Fayoum seemed haunted by the shadowy presence of some 600 models whose funeral portraits line the walls of

European museums. ❦ Shortly after the train crossed the Nile, there was Luxor with its temples and the 20 or so sanctuaries of Karnak. On the opposite bank were the ancient city of Thebes, the Valley of the Kings and the tomb of Tutankhamen whose treasures had been excavated in 1922 and now lay in Cairo Museum. Next came Aswan, with its islands, the black rocks of the Elephantine, and legendary island of Philae, sacred birthplace of the goddess Isis. This deserved a stay in the Hôtel Cataracte before continuing up to Cairo among the crocodiles and the feluccas, on board one of those paddle steamers launched by Thomas Cook. ❦ Those arriving in Egypt by sea had to go across country through the Biblical Lands. It was 381 miles by train from Cairo to Haifa then 156 miles by car from Syria to Tripoli where they would board the train once again. In Aleppo, there was a connection for Baghdad – and its port, Basra, on the Persian Gulf and the doorway to India. Everything passed through Aleppo, including the Calcutta to Stockholm

car rally. ❦ With the railway completed, it took just seven days to travel to Cairo from London, eight days from Baghdad. The distance was always calculated from London because Syria and Mesopotamia were teeming with English archaeologists, such as one Professor Max Mallowan who would marry an English writer of whodunits called Agatha Christie. Horsepower now replaced the horses of a wild-eyed Anglo-Irish colonel called Lawrence who gave up his rank to become Lawrence of Arabia . . . ❦ The route from Aleppo to London lay through the Cicilian Gates – a pass on the road to every conquest since before Alexander the Great – over the snowy peaks of the Taurus Mountains, across the Bosporus and then finally across the English Channel. According to the newspapers, it was planned to build tunnels under both. In the meantime passengers boarded the CIWI launch for Istanbul in Haydar Pacha from which point the trip on the *Orient-Express* would be almost humdrum. ❦ In the far south, the Middle East was merely a place that came after the Midi in France and Marseilles "the capital of the Empire." Or as Marseilles journalist Méry put it, "Africa is a suburb, India is on the outskirts, America is a neighbor." From 1927 onward, passengers arrived in Marseilles on the *Paris-Lyon-Méditerranée*, passed down the majestic staircase of the Gare Saint Charles past a statue of a reclining African woman, naked but for her bracelets and anklets: symbol of the willing

colonies. ✃ From Marseilles there were daily departures for Oran, Algiers, Philippeville, Bône and Tunis with the *Compagnie Générale Transatlantique*. The C.G.T.-owned *Ville d'Alger* was "the fastest in the Mediterranean," as fast as the transatlantic lines, steaming from Paris to Algiers via Marseilles in 33 hours. The ticket, whether leaving from Paris or London, covered travel by boat and train. ✃ In North Africa, the C.G.T. took charge of everything and offered "car trips" for 15 people in long convertible limousines. In 1929 more than 5,000 tourists traveled in its 288 vehicles and stayed in its 44 hotels – although the word "hotel" can hardly do justice to the Palais de la Mamounia that the C.G.T. was creating at vast expense in Marrakech. ✃ There were also crossings from Marseilles to Tangier in Morocco, where the painter Eugène Delacroix traveled. Casablanca was reached from Bordeaux: the train journey from the Gare d'Orsay in Paris to the port of Bordeaux took seven hours; the sea crossing to Casablanca took three days. The borders of Morocco and the southern region of Oran were still humming with the exploits of an intrepid young Russian woman called Isabelle Eberhardt. Disguised as a man, and a soldier to boot, she took the name of Si Mahmouhd and traveled to the Atlas Mountains in the Sahara before tragically disappearing in the Ksour Mountains at Ain Sefra. ✃ The future was wide open. Casablanca had not yet become a dead end place where all you did was wait for a boat to the New World; a place where, in Rick's American Bar, Ingrid Bergman told the black pianist to "Play it, Sam. Play "As time goes by". . . I'll hum it for you. That nostalgic tune of happy times spent in Paris with Humphrey Bogart.

Alain Rustenholz

Above: 1930s poster for the Moroccan-based Compagnie Générale des Transports de Tourisme (C.T.M. - General Tourism Transport Company). Left: luggage label for the Hotel Plaza, Casablanca, Morocco. Right: photographic souvenirs of trips across the Mediterranean between 1890 and 1930 to Casablanca, to Constantine …. Previous pages: original documents recalling the Messageries Maritimes (the major shipping line to the East).

Pages from an 1895 brochure and the cover of an elegant album extolling the region around Algiers and Blida (p. 118); Port Said, c. 1890 (p. 119, top); the Victoria Hotel on the route to Damascus, ancient Palestine, c. 1900 (p. 119, bottom); the Great Pyramid of Cheops, c. 1880 (photo by J. P. Sebah, p. 120); and a C.I.W.L. poster promoting eastern travel (p. 121).

de la porte Bab-el-Djebbiah.

Constantine

Constantine – Marchands d'oranges.

Constantine – Me

12 - CASABLANCA – Place de France

ياحة والاصطياف
إدارية - سورتا

FROM THE WINDOW OF MY HOTEL BEDROOM OVERLOOKING THE OLD PORT, I gazed absently mindedly at the seething cosmopolitan population. In the haze of gold dust that was whipped up by a light mistral, people and things had a vaguely mirage-like appearance. [...] in spirit I had already crossed the "threshold" and landed in India . . . . .

Alexandra David-Néel, 1951

Left: The Canebière Boulevard on the seafront, a pier on dry land in the Vieux-Port. This was the home of the Stock Exchange – the "Louvre of Commerce" – and its Colonial Institute, and also the location of the big Marseilles cafés like the Turkish café described by Théophile Gautier; the Grand Café Glacier right on the corner of the Place de la Bourse; the Café de la Paix where people met to discuss business; the cafés-concerts where you mixed with the riff-raff; the gaming circles . . . .

Right: The Vieux-Port. It was to Marseilles that Rimbaud returned to die and from Marseilles that Paul Eluard set sail for Tahiti in 1924. André Gaillard meanwhile admired the "mails [...], ravishers of golden apples and bearers of dreams, advancing at full sail towards the Garden of the Hesperides." And Louis Brauquier wrote: "I feel a sad sense of anguish. To have watched others depart and not to have left . . . ."

THERE IS THE MIDDAY SILENCE ON THE PLACE DU GOUVERNEMENT. In the shade of the trees that line it, Arabs sell glasses of iced lemonade flavored with orange flowers for five sous. The deserted square echoes with their cries of "Cool, cool". […] There is the silence of the siesta. In the streets of the Marine, it is measurable by the melodious buzzing of the flies behind the beaded curtains at the entrance to the grimy hairdressing salons. Elsewhere, in the Moorish cafés of the Kasbah, it is the body that is silent, that cannot tear itself away from this place, leave the glass of tea and return to time and the sounds of life. Mainly though there is the silence of summer nights.

Albert Camus, 1959

The port of Algiers in the 1930s (above): blue-fish fishermen (tuna, sardines, anchovies) with the seafront in the background and the boulevard resting on its arcades that served as warehouses. Until 1914, most of the visitors to Algiers were English people. These "winter tourists" as they were known at the time could take their pick from no less than seven grand hotels situated on the Heights of Mustapha, not to mention the countless specially built villas. They had their own newspaper, the Algerian Advertiser, their own church, an Anglican chaplain and a Scots Presbyterian minister.

The cathedral on Government Square (right) with its air of Moorish style. Camille Saint-Saëns played the organ there; he would also give his last piano recital at the Algiers Opera House. Following double-page display: page from a photograph album belonging to a non-commissioned-officer of the 1891 levy that served in Algeria. It shows the petrified waterfall of the Hamman of Meskoutine, together with a detailed hand-written description of this astonishing place situated between Bône and Constantine. "Every spring, military and civilian bathers come to be cured in the waters of the Hamman Meskoutine. The deposits in the waterfalls, with their stalactites, needles, frozen folds, graceful pools, multitude of tones ranging from the purest milky white to a light rust color, all crowned in columns of vapor – all these create an extremely beautiful picture."
Insert: scenes from Maghreb the Eternal showing camel drivers pausing in the desert.
Previous double-page display: steam ship arriving in the Port of Algiers c. 1910.

...ouve l'entrée des grottes de Faïa, qu'on ... ...fer, mais que le touriste fera bien à ... ...un viaduc du chemin de fer, à une d[istance]... ...dessus du Bou-Hamdan se trouvent les... ...rain, une splendide. En deux heures... ...de la nécropole celtique de Roknia... ...es d'Announa du côté opposé. ... ...spéciale à Hamma-Meskoutine... ...et puissant avait une sœur; mais la... ...ancer à un autre qu'à lui, voulut... ...melle de la loi musulmane, malgré... ...ations des anciens de la tribu, dont... ...tente. Alors commencèrent les fantasias... ...n immense festin, puis, comme le... ...rev, les éléments furent bouleversés... ...lit de terre, les eaux de leur lit... ...ablement; puis quand tout rev... ...ouja l'Arabe et sa sœur, les gens... ...useuses et les esclaves pétrifiés;... ...es auteurs de ce drame. Si, s... ...ésonne sous les pieds des chevaux... ...le de la noce. Si l'une des sources... ...au dehors des corps ronds ou ov... ...és drayées, les indigènes ne man... ...e que ces petits corps, pisoli... ...olonne liquide contenant des sel... ...rains de Kouskoussou du repas des... ...lo, quand vient la nuit, fuyez cett... ...e reprend sa forme, la noce recom... ...ontinuer et malheur à celui qui... ...: Quand le jour reviendrait il... ...re de cônes. (Docteur Hamel).

Hamma

skoutine _ Cascade d'eau chaude.

de la gare de Hamma
rougeant d'abord le petit hôpita
end à travers de beaux massif
ascade pétrifiée. Au delà à
aux militaires et l

COMPAGNIE GÉNÉRALE
TRANSATLANTIQUE
& CHEMINS DE FER
PARIS-LYON-MÉDITERRANÉE

MEANWHILE AT THE END OF THE PLAIN, AT THE POINT WHERE THE LOWERING SKY WAS AT ITS LOWEST, the yellowish sun suddenly revealed its presence in long rays cast through the deep shadows where we stood; [...] As I looked, disoriented and undecided, at that distant pale rip in the sky, a procession of large creatures walked past the sun; slow, swaying creatures whose long legs cast endlessly extended shadows over the plain: the African caravans!

Pierre Loti, 1889

"The city is almost entirely surrounded by a second wall composed of gardens of palm and olive trees that are so close in places that they actually touch the city walls and the palm trees lean their heads on the dilapidated battlements," wrote the brothers Tharaud.

Above: left, a palm grove near Marrakech and, right, Djema el Fna Square, "Square of Death" for some, "Meeting place of Miracles" for others. With the minaret of Koutoubia overlooking the scene some 20 yards away, a car draws the crowds that usually gather round the storytellers, dancers and snake charmers.

Following double-page display: the *souk* (market) in Marrakech in the 1990s. "Next to a dark, shady hole stands a brightly varnished mahogany closet " wrote Henriette Célarié in 1923. "Streaks of gold highlight corners that never see the light of day. A scrap of silk glistens . . . ." In 1930 Raymond Boissier added "copper pans glow at the back of dark stores, glinting yellow through the semi-darkness and sprinkling the dusty shadows with errant sparks . . . ."

Previous double-page display: North African travel, c. 1910. Passengers from France traveled with the P.L.M (Paris-Lyon-Mediterranean) and the C.G.T. Once there, they could explore by caravan or in one of the newly launched C.T.M tourist buses.

AFTER THE DELIGHTFUL GARDEN CAME A CORRIDOR WHERE I COULD HERE THE SOUND OF GUSHING WATER FROM THE ENTRANCE, and then finally I reached the large inner courtyard [...]: it was paved with mosaics made up of thousands of tiny blue, yellow, black and white designs that glistened with moisture; [...] water gushed from a white marble basin in the center and from an exquisite wall-mounted fountain at the side. The apartments that opened onto this courtyard had immense doors of solid oak.

Pierre Loti, 1889

The terrace (left) and the grand lounge (right) of the Palas-Hôtel de la Mamounia in Marrakech. First there was a garden full of banana, orange and lemon trees whose fruits punctuated the dark, glossy greenery with touches of brightness. The light filtered gently through the slender, silvery leaves of 300-year-old olive trees and the air was fragrant with the scent of large saffron roses. Eventually a palace was built around the garden, gracing it with "the most exquisite shoulders and the most beautiful jewels" and orchestras playing music by Ravel and Granados. In 1986 the Mamounia was renovated to a high standard of luxury in accordance with the rather flashy notion of "international taste."

THE CITY OF PORT SAID IS LIKE A HUGE BAZAAR or caravansary, where people of all origins seem to meet for brief, furtive encounters and the very appearance of the companies is enough to convey the cosmopolitan nature of a city that hardly qualifies as Egyptian at all despite being on Egyptian soil [...]. Passers-by are accosted in the street and offered the most extraordinary collection of things. There is a flourishing trade in postage stamps, for instance [...] Cut-price Egyptian cigarettes are offered to all and sundry. Cigars may also be sampled by unsuspecting customers who struggle in vain to light twisted bunches of badly dried tobacco leaves that reek of French *infectados*.

F. Lagrillière-Beauclerc, 1900

With its pioneering appearance, Port Said was a makeshift trading post. The aptly named Rue du Commerce (left) represented firms from every corner of the globe. Right: the verandah outside Shepheard's Hotel in Cairo (photo by Bonfils, c. 1880), a place on the margin between shade and fierce sunlight, where two worlds exchanged views and East met West. The turbans and tunics of the working classes mingled with the European suits and Turkish fezzes of the elite and veiled women rubbed shoulders with elegant Parisian ladies. People arrived at Shepheard's, stayed at Shepheard's and departed from Shepheard's: for the Pyramids, in barouches and victorias driven by black cabbies from Nubia or the Sudan, and on donkeys to the bazaar.

Following double-page display: the grandiose dining-room of the Heliopolis Palace Hotel that at the end of 1910 – as if grafted from a casino – sprang up out of a new, rectilinear district in the desert. It was a far cry from Bedouin cloaks, whirling dervishes and Coptic crypts that, in keeping with local tradition, sheltered the Virgin and Child. Inset: Shepheard's Hotel baggage label.

SHE AND HER SON WERE SITTING IN BRIGHTLY PAINTED SCARLET BASKET CHAIRS outside the Cataract Hotel in Assuan. They were watching the retreating figures of two people - a short man dressed in a white silk suit and a tall slim girl. [...]. They turned to the left out of the hotel gate and entered the [...] public gardens. [...] "...It enchants me," he was saying. "The black rocks of the Elephantine, and the sun, and the little boats on the river ...

Agatha Christie, 1948

Heliopolis - Terrace of the Heliopolis House Hotel.

Left: the letter-writing ceremony on the terrace of the Heliopolis Hotel and of a hotel in Helwan (right), a spa town that was famous at the start of the 20th century. A journey was something to be described, a story to be told as it happened. Like this missionary's wife describing her visit to the bazaar: " 'I suppose you tell the truth around once a year?' I inquired of one of the few merchants who could speak English properly. 'No, ma'am, twice' he replied."
Insert: Heliopolis Hotel luggage label.

Is it a mountain of sand that we see before us? There is no way of telling because it has no contours as such; the impression it creates is more of a large pink cloud, a large wave of barely substantial water that rose up in times gone by and stayed frozen there forever … Emerging from that apparently mummified wave, also pink, of an indescribable, almost fleeting pink, a colossal human effigy raises its head, gazes fixedly and smiles; […]. And behind its monstrous face, much further back, at the top of those vague, softly undulating dunes, three apocalyptic signs rise up into the sky, three pink triangles as regular as geometric designs but so enormous as to look frightening from a distance..

Pierre Loti, 1907

GIZA

People climbed onto camels to have their photograph taken in front of the Sphinx then climbed down to climb onto the Sphinx and have their photographs taken again. "That strange old Minx" as it was called by an English tourist who made an interesting slip of the tongue . . . .
Following double-page display: on the banks of the Nile c. 1880 (photo by J. P. Sebah). The Pyramids usually seemed much smaller from the road, much smaller than the huge mountains people expected. Their true dimensions only became apparent as people approached on foot and went up to touch them. The Mena House Hotel is practically at the foot of Cheops' Pyramid, visible to guests from their beds on moonlit nights.

ARRIVED IN KARNAK along the grand avenue with the mutilated sphinxes and the monumental column in the west Magnificent entrance. On the right, view of the column intact on the north side and crumbling on the south side. The great temple. Remarkable sight. Huge dimensions. Need a ladder to measure them. Nothing more gigantic or more solemn. Things crumbling on all sides, a huge pile of rubble made up of monstrous blocks of stone. Segments of column bathing in holes that are still full of water. Four obelisks, but only two still standing.

Eugène Fromentin, 1869

Thebes was the capital of all Egypt for half a century 2,000 years before the present era. Now it lies buried under modern-day Luxor (right, photo by Bonfils). The Winter Palace Hotel in Luxor is only open in the winter months in the brief tourist season. The Prince of Wales – fifth from the left on the photo above – almost delayed his schedule for this shot taken by Sir Francis Bedford's camera on 16 March 1862. Inset: Winter Palace baggage label.
Following double-page display: left, the colossal statue of Amenophis III (photo by P. M. Good, c. 1860) erroneously referred to by the Greeks and Romans as the "Colossus of Memnon." Following

their partial collapse, the stones warmed by the sun were heard to "sing" and people said it was Memnon greeting her mother, Aurora. Hence the nickname of the "singing statue." The phenomenon came to an end in 170 AD when Septimius Severus ordered the statue to be restored – proving that even the Ancients were capable of making a mess of things . . . . On 25 March 1852, Maxime du Camp himself arranged for the rubble to be cleared from the western colossus of Abu Simbel (right, photo by P. M. Good) that had almost entirely collapsed under a pile of debris. Du Camp took measurements, including the size of the nostrils, and also tried to take rubbings of the bas-reliefs and inscriptions – although not of the graffiti we can see in this picture. The day before, these surroundings had inspired his friend the writer Flaubert with the name of the heroine for his next book: Emma Bovary. The name had nothing to do with Egypt of course, which just goes to show that there are a thousand different ways of traveling.

No sound of a car in that gloomy city, not a person in sight, just the peal of bells ringing through the air. The lanes are as narrow as deep, bottomless ditches. No flowers or gardens. Here and there, a solitary cypress tree in a bare courtyard surrounded by empty arcades. Tightly packed houses with hardly any windows [...] Parapets on the terraces crowned by small cupolas. The eye is drawn however to two enormous black domes that tower above the others. The one standing in the center of town is the Sacred Sepulcher or Tomb of Christ. The other occupying the site of Solomon's temple in the southwest corner is the Mosque of Omar or the Tomb of Jehovah (sic). And so the houses of the living disappear, crushed by these tombs of the gods.

Edouard Schuré, 1898

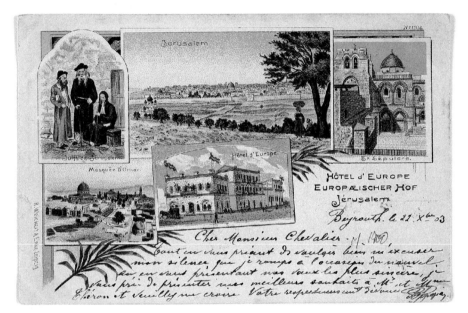

Jewish New Year greetings written by a French tourist on a Hôtel d'Europe postcard in Jerusalem (above) and posted in Beirut on 2 October 1903.
Right: the Armenian church in the Armenian quarter of Jerusalem (photo by Bonfils c. 1880). When Palestine was under British rule, there were three other quarters in Jerusalem: the Christian or Frankish quarter, the Moslem quarter and the Jewish quarter.

Following double-page display: "photo souvenir" of a group of tourists and their guides in full traditional costume, taken at the foot of the walls of Jerusalem on 29 December 1900. The names of this happy band of travelers appear on the back of the photo and include a French couple, an American couple from Kansas City and an English couple from Brighton. The "scout" and the *dragoman* (official interpreter, second from the right in the front row) complete this family portrait!

Oo the horizon, still some distance away, on the first foothills of the black mountains facing the Lebanon, an immense group of yellow ruins burnished by the setting sun stood out against the shade of the mountains [.... Our guides pointed them out to us shouting: "Baalbek! Baalbek!" It was indeed that wonder of the desert, the fabulous Baalbek, triumphantly emerging from her unknown tomb to tell us of ages past that are lost in history. We advanced slowly keeping pace with our tired horses [...]: a profound silence reigned throughout the caravan; so afraid was everyone of missing what the hour had to express that none would communicate the impression he had just received.

Lamartine, 1832

LEBANON

The acropolis in Baalbek, c. 1900 (above): six columns on the southern flank are all that remain of the 19 columns that used to grace the long walls of the Temple of Jupiter Heliopolitain that was completed under Nero or Vespasian. Farther right are the remains of the 2nd-century temple known as the Temple of Bacchus. To the west is Mount Lebanon rising to nearly 10,000 feet.
Right: a *dragoman* (photo by Bonfils, c. 1880). The word refers to interpreters in Moslem countries from the Levant to Constantinople who were officially responsible for backing up diplomatic and consular agents. The term "interpreter" was reserved for agents working in the Far East. By extension *"dragoman"* came to mean a mediator between two cultures. One of those invaluable guides was Nicola Bassoul, founder of the Grand Hôtel d'Orient in Beirut, known more simply as the Bassoul Hotel (following double-page display). On the left is the bar, on the right is the grand oriental lounge, photographed here c. 1980. The desk and chest, dated 1892, are of precious wood inlaid with ivory and pearls. Insert: baggage label from the Hôtel St-Georges, one of the most famous hotels in Beirut in the first half of the 20th century.

Menu

Consomme Celestin

Trancons de Barbel d'Euphrate Maitre d'Hotel

Medaillon de Veau Bourguignonne
Petits Pois a la Parisienne
Pommes Marquis

Bombe Alaska

Cafe

Diner du 27 Juin 1937.

Hotel Baron,
Alep, Syrie.

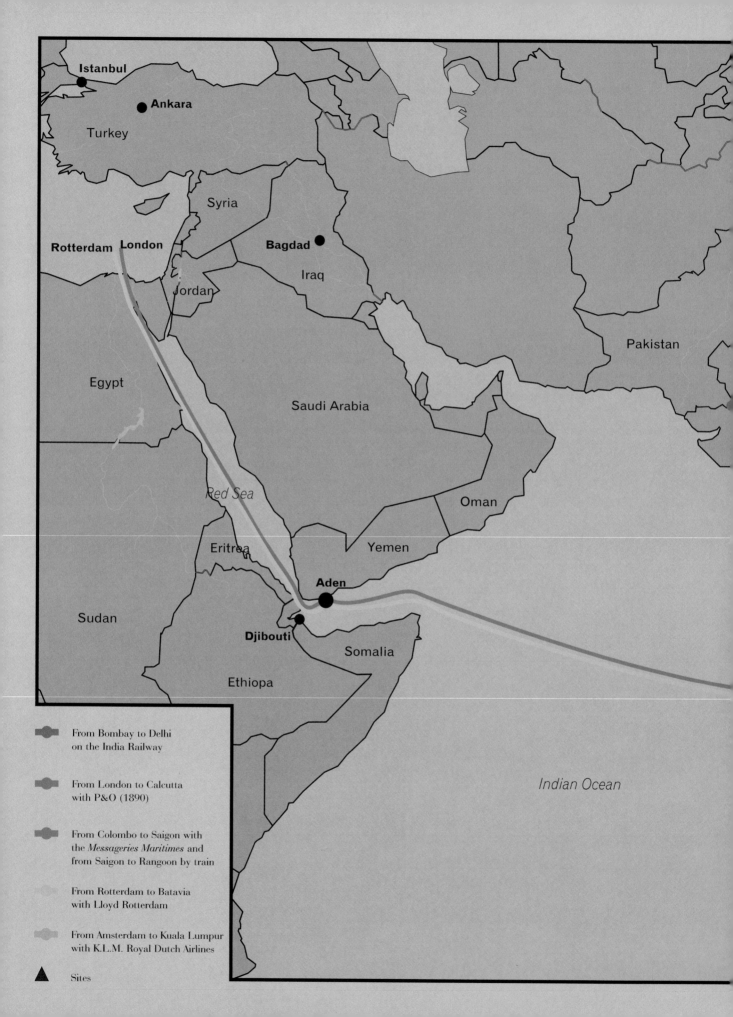

Istanbul

Ankara

Turkey

Syria

Rotterdam London

Bagdad

Jordan

Iraq

Egypt

Saudi Arabia

Red Sea

Eritrea

Oman

Yemen

Aden

Sudan

Djibouti

Somalia

Ethiopa

Pakistan

Indian Ocean

From Bombay to Delhi
on the India Railway

From London to Calcutta
with P&O (1890)

From Colombo to Saigon with
the *Messageries Maritimes* and
from Saigon to Rangoon by train

From Rotterdam to Batavia
with Lloyd Rotterdam

From Amsterdam to Kuala Lumpur
with K.L.M. Royal Dutch Airlines

Sites

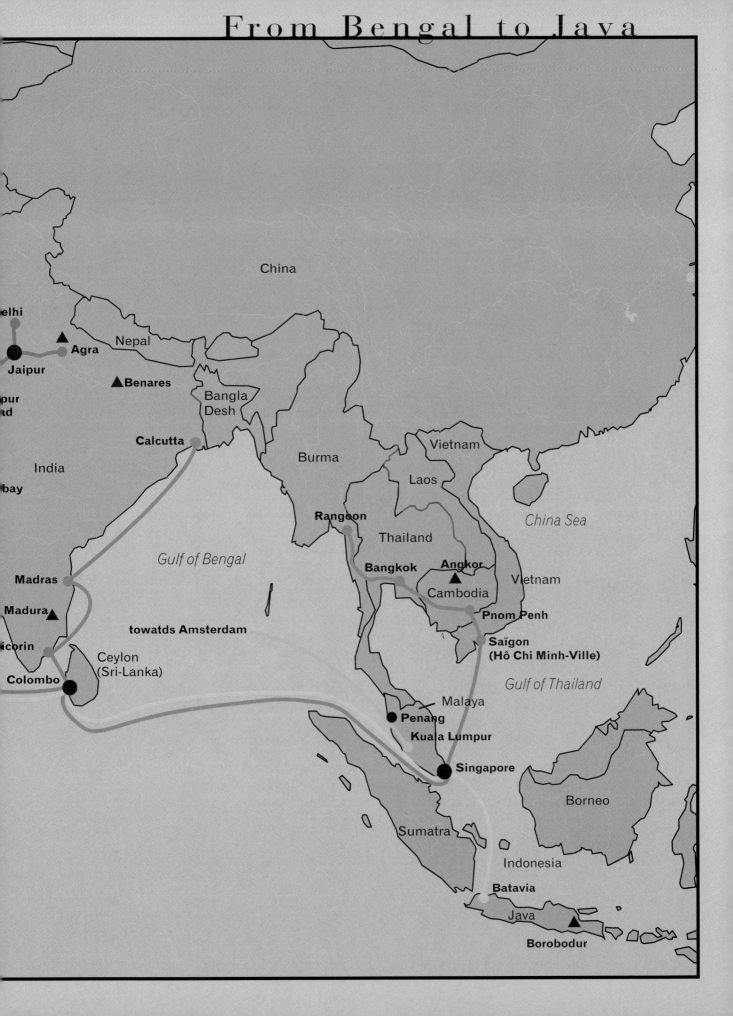

China

Nepal

▲ Agra

Jaipur

▲ Benares

Bangla
Desh

Calcutta

Vietnam

India

Burma

Laos

bay

Rangoon

China Sea

Gulf of Bengal

Thailand

Bangkok

▲ Angkor

Cambodia

Vietnam

Madras

Pnom Penh

Madura ▲

towatds Amsterdam

Saïgon
(Hô Chi Minh-Ville)

icorin

Ceylon
(Sri-Lanka)

Gulf of Thailand

Colombo

Malaya

● Penang

Kuala Lumpur

● Singapore

Borneo

Sumatra

Indonesia

Batavia

Java

Borobodur

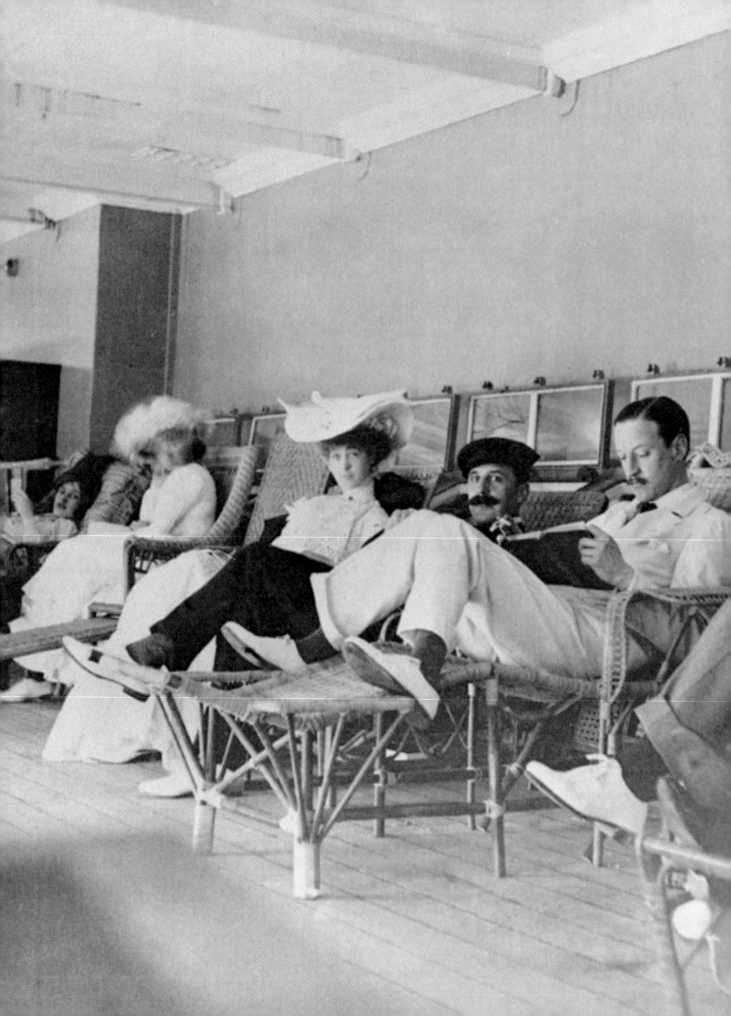

Journeys further afield than Suez were measured in weeks rather than days. There were also stopovers where passengers could look at something other than the ship itself. For those traveling with the British P & O Line — which since it had supported the Portuguese and Spanish crowns during their respective civil uprisings in the 1830s, flew a surprising flag combining the blue and white of Portugal with the red and yellow of Spain - there was a chance of meeting fabulous Indian Maharajahs. Holy Ganges water for their ritual ablutions always traveled with them in silver urns. On the French ships meanwhile, North African pilgrims traveling to Mecca had to make do with water from vulgar barrels covered with makeshift awnings on deck. Despite that, the French lines irrespective of destination were popular with foreigners for gastronomic reasons. ❦ Port Said, a five-day crossing from Marseilles, was but the gateway to a canal

between three continents and the place where the pilot boarded the ship. On deck, this was where everyone changed into their whites and all the passengers suddenly looked like colonials. ❦ Five days later the ship sailed out of the Red Sea into Aden, a free port at the foot of a fierce citadel called Djibouti. Aden was where India began and the British resident answered to British administration in Bombay. In Djibouti, coins rained from the decks of French ships entering the port and suddenly the sea was awash with "soles of feet that were more or less white floating on the water like bizarre lily-pads": the feet of the lads who jumped in to seize the change in their teeth like ducks diving for bread. ❦ This is where several routes crossed. Bombay lay opposite, reached simply by sailing up the southern coast of Arabia: Bombay and its islands, groaning under merchandise that was transported as much by land as by sea. Or there were the railways: southeast via Hyderabad down to Madras; eastwards, towards the Ganges valley and Calcutta; northwards down to Delhi via Udaipur, Jaipur and Agra. ❦ By 1843 however, when mail from England was still being sent overland to Egypt, P&O ships were already linking Suez to Calcutta. Their route lay around Cape Comorin, passing between Ceylon and the Coromandel Coast and straight into the Gulf of Bengal. In seven days, you were in Ceylon where there was stop-over in Colombo, a Garden of Eden where you could take a rickshaw up to Mount Lavinia to admire the sun setting on the ocean. Then, hugging the shore to the Adam's Bridge, you set off again for Madura where the palace predating Versailles was a masterpiece of civil engineering in southern India. Finally you reached Calcutta, capital of British India until 1911 and comprising the European city around Fort William — that guarded the magnificent university — and the teeming Indian city. ❦ Those who took the train from Bombay might have passed the Viceroy of

India's train, a long dazzlingly white snake within which you sometimes caught a glimpse of the Sovereign in his equally dazzlingly uniform. In Udaipur, you would have seen the magnificent palace of the Maharani and the Hindu temple of Jagannatha. You would also have passed through Jaipur, ancient religious capital of the Orissa and still a place of pilgrimage; Agra and the Taj Mahal, weeping precious stones; Delhi that succeeded Calcutta as the capital of India, with its Koutab, Mughal palace and narrow streets lined with brick-built houses. ℭ Back in the Indian Ocean, there were the Sunda Islands in the Dutch East Indies where the jagged outlines of the volcanoes of Java tower over the tip of the temple of the 500 Buddhas of Borobudur. Barely visible on the horizon, the temple is said to house the ashes of the last king of Mataram who, rumor has it, died of pleasure entombed in his palace with his 6,000 wives. Gauguin, who liked to dip his brush into the waters around Tahiti and the Marquesas Islands, nevertheless chose two views of Borobudur as decoration for his straw hut. Sumatra, the neighboring island, bristled with sandalwood and teak: for many years the casings in the *Wagon-Lits* were made of teak and there was a hotel on the Pacific built entirely of sandalwood. Imagine a bedroom with perfumed walls — but let's leave that for another journey.. ℭ Still further east, was Singapore on the banks of the Straits of Malacca: "The Straits of Malacca are the corridor to the Equator. They seem to absorb all the heat of the planet that then spreads to the rest of the world. The sea is like a huge steaming kettle and the tropical humidity is exhausting, draining and enervating," comments Roland Dorgelès. Fortunately, there was Raffles Hotel, with its cocoon-like European climate created by an impressive battery of fans . . . . Moments away, caught between the tin mines and hevea plantations, was Kuala Lumpur which built a station in the shape of a mosque but made way for Chinese temples and Victorian architecture. ℭ Veering northwards, there was Burma, Marco Polo's "Kingdom of Mien," or there was Thailand. How paradoxical to arrive by train in Rangoon, the third major port on the Indian Ocean after Calcutta and Bombay. There was no shortage of reasons to go to Bangkok if only to recapture what Louise Weiss describes in *Mémoires d'une Européenne*: "In his youth, the delightful old

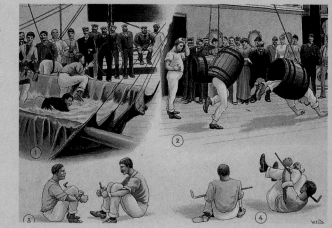

à l'arrière
du *Touraine*

1907

TROPICAL HOLLAND
THE ARCHIPELAGO OF ETERNAL SUMMER

diplomat had fallen passionately in love with a young girl who had turned him down to enter a convent. He never stopped cherishing her memory, however. Determined and secretive, he had secured a post in Bangkok where she was the Mother Superior of a flourishing Carmelite community. Once there, he had applied his diplomatic talents to persuading the Emperor of Siam to visit the convent. According to the rules of the Order, only a sovereign could demand to be admitted to the enclosure. The tower opened for the Monarch. The diplomat who accompanied him noticed his sweetheart and greeted her, beside himself with joy. They exchanged not a word. Only looks. Then the doors of the convent closed once again." Other reasons to go to Bangkok included the Wat-Cheng pagoda and the former royal palace. There was also Angkor with its Indian and Brahman art dating from our age of the cathedrals. that the Ecole Française d'Extrême-Orient was busy rescuing from the forest. In Pnom-Penh, the recent capital, the only pyramid shapes to be seen were those on the ceremonial head-dresses. ✲ In Saigon, people whiled away the hours on the terrace of the Continental, alongside the Rue Catinat where the whole town came to life from six in the evening to two in the morning. Imagine Roland Dorgelès about to leave the Continental where he has just set one of the scenes in his next book, *Sur la Route Mandarine*; Graham Greene, the Times war correspondent, is shortly to arrive. And so, after countless articles in the press, pedal-powered rickshaws gradually replaced man-hauled rickshaws on the Rue Catinat . . . .

Alain Rustenholz

Above: 1930s poster adverting the Dutch East Indies, "The Archipelago of Eternal Summer"; left: luggage label for the Djokjakarta Hotel; right: one of the statues of the Buddha on the upper levels of the temple of Borobudur in Java. Previous pages: the Duke of Marlborough and his family on board the P&O ship Arabia in 1902 (p. 166); in the corridors of the Lake Palace in Udaipur in 1987 (p. 167); Russian diplomatic delegation arriving in Hanoi around 1890 (p. 168, above); games and other activities on board a P&O ship in 1870 (p. 168, below); drawing from a watercolor album belonging to a member of the crew; *"At the rear of the Tourane"* in 1909, shot taken from an anonymous family photograph album (p. 169); and a baggage label for the Continental Hotel in Saigon, featuring the celebrated "Bengal Tiger."

KANDY IS A SMALL, CHARACTERISTICALLY INDIAN TOWN. [...] The narrow streets lined with low houses come to life at daybreak. [...] Trip into the mountains in very agreeable company. We took the train that would eventually link Kandy to the highest part of the island. It was made up of a great many carriages full of local people for whom traveling by train was a real pleasure. [...] The tracks wound steadily upwards, parallel to the road that was suitable for motor vehicles [...]. The higher you went, the less tropical the vegetation became. The air was pure, cool and buoyant. You forgot that you were on the sixth parallel of latitude.

Count Joseph von Hübner, 1886

No sooner had the ship dropped anchor in the port of Colombo than the stewards of the Oriental Hotel (above) and those of the Galle Face – whose giant palm trees festooned with multicolored lights were visible from the ship – were already on board taking charge of the luggage. Coolies meanwhile escorted guests to the hotel, pushing their rickshaws through the gem sellers and the ivory sellers, the pendant sellers and the sellers of wooden elephants with emerald trunks, past the boots of the English, the bright tunics of the Sinhalese and the velvet skullcaps of the Malaysians.
Left: the winding railway to Kandy, ancient royal capital of the island with a small lake in the center where elephants were taken at bath time.
Following double-page display: the temple of the Tooth of the Buddha and a monk in saffron robes surrounded by red hibiscus flowers, gigantic rhododendrons, royal poincianas humming with hummingbirds, hundreds of pink butterflies, small zebus with painted horns, mango trees, date-palms with spindly trunks and equally spindly areca nut trees.

FROM THE DEPTHS OF THE ANCIENT PLAIN WHERE THE GANGES FLOWS, from the depths of that immense plain of silt and grazing lands that the night's vapors shroud ever more thickly in mist, the eternal sun has just risen as it has risen every day for three thousand years. There before it, blocking its first pink ray, are the granite surfaces of Benares with its red pyramids and golden peaks, the entire holy city arranged like an amphitheater as if greedily seizing first light and basking in the glory of the morning.

Pierre Loti, 1903

In Benares, *ghats* or stairways in the riverbank lead to landing stages that serve as places of ablution and cremation. This city of the dispossessed is also a center of rich fabrics, silks, cottons and cloth; this city of destitution also dazzles with pomp and ceremony laden with flowers, fruit and lights; this city of holiness is also a place of letters that has been home to a Sanskrit school since the end of the 18th century. Everything converges on the Ganges and its holy waters, flowing with virtues that pilgrims try to take with them when they leave. In 1910 Calcutta was already bursting at the seams, a city of seething populations where holiness in its most humble form was an intimate part of everyday life: the sacred cow. Following double-page display: the Botanical Garden in Calcutta in 1872 where the ferocious, invasive jungle was kept carefully in check. The waterfalls tumbled rather than roared and all the plants were neatly aligned – mango trees, royal poincianas with scarlet flowers, jacquiers with huge fruits sometimes weighing 50 lbs., giant bamboo, guava trees, evergreen cinnamon trees fragrant with spice and coconut trees – were neatly aligned. Visitors were strictly forbidden to stray from the smoothly raked path so there was no danger here of unwisely falling asleep forever beneath the tree "whose shade means death." Insert: 1931 promotional leaflet for P&O.

SANSI OPENED THE DOOR AND STEPPED BACK A 100 YEARS IN TIME. The room was large with white walls, high vaulted ceilings and fluted columns crowned with gold leaf. The furniture was old, opulent and dark. One wall was curved and accommodated a series of small windows that gave a breathtaking view of the mountains, the lake and the sprawling blue city ... below.

Paul Mann, 1998

You reached Udaipur across rice paddies and cotton fields where suddenly, there in the water, young shoots made way for small columns and downy cotton balls were replaced by polished marble. The royal palaces were lakeside-pile dwellings that stood on their islets like sugar cakes on cake stands, studded with bright flowers and black crows. Above and right: the City Palace, the second of Udaipur's royal palaces to be converted into a hotel. The view on the left shows the palace in 1880, the one on the right gives an idea of the atmosphere that reigns there to this day: "Countless courtyards fragrant with giant orange trees that flower between white marble arches! Vestibules trailing with oriental slippers; men with long swords sitting in every corner!" (Pierre Loti, *L'Inde sans les Anglais*).

Following double-page display: the Lake Palace Hotel, home of the Maharajah in the18th century, also opened to mere mortals, offering its ceremonial boats to visitors who could relax on the softly undulating water, fanned by gentle breezes. The love swing (following pages), symbol of other pleasures that occasionally swung in time to the *Kamasutra*, was always positioned directly in line with the sun, swinging between sunrise and sunset.

WITH MUCH BOWING AND SCRAPING, A PORTER IMMEDIATELY LED US to an immense apartment located in the old building with a terrace that gave onto an inner garden and balconies overlooking the sea. Your feet sank at least six inches into thick carpet that was white as snow. The bathroom was as tall as a cathedral nave and two hippopotamuses could have splashed around in the bath. The closets had been designed for a theater wardrobe, supermen could have slept in the beds and the three of us occupied enough space to accommodate an entire village [...]. The air was cooled by dozens of giant fans that roared like fighter planes. If they were all switched on at once, there was a positive sirocco blowing through the room with things flying all over the place. Sheets flapped and billowed, pillows clacked like jibs on mainsails, socks glided through the air like feathers, doors slammed, walls bowed and even your hair stood on end.

Pascal Brückner, 1985

Above left: the Bycullah Hotel in Bombay in 1871.
Right: the dome of the Taj Hotel in Bombay has overlooked the port and the P&O landing stages (right) since the 1900s. In a moving encounter, the endlessly bobbing lines of the boats harmonize with the lines on the varied façade of the hotel. Against a gray-blue background of sea and granite, the gaze darts from an arch to a lintel, a bow window to a vault, the ball on a cupola to the sharp corner of a roof.
Although the Taj was built as a hotel, the grand stairway beneath the dome and the majestic ballroom were grand enough for the receptions held by the Maharajah of Alwar.
Following double-page display: the rattan lounge on the terrace of the Taj. The chessboard on the table serves as a reminder that chess originated in India where it was apparently invented to teach a young king a lesson in democracy. Given that this particular palace is open to the public, the chessboard shown here could not be more appropriate.

us Maharaja Alwar
(Je Isinghji) of Alwar

TONIGHT AT SUNSET THE SUN IS STILL SHINING AS THE LITTLE LIGHTS GO ON all around the great temple of Madura, along the vaulted granite avenue that is like a sort of entrance hall where the garland sellers gather. For someone like me coming from outside, everything became indistinguishable in the sudden half-light: men confused with idols and monsters, human faces with oversize stone faces, the frozen gestures of people with too many arms mistaken for the real movements of people with only two. There are also the sacred cows [...] lingeringly chewing the rushes and flowers before going into the temple to sleep.

Pierre Loti, 1900

The room in the west wing of the Karikai Thotti Palace Hotel (left) where the last Maharajah of Mysore received official visitors: Hindu-style carved wooden pillars that are 10 ft apart in every direction support Hindu-style carved wooden arches. The furnishings meanwhile are essentially European.
Right: a smaller temple housing a divinity next to one of the four cardinal doors (located at the four main points of the compass) with pyramidal roofs (*gopura*) that belong to the temple of Madura. Foreigners and the lower castes are not allowed within the enclosure but Brahmans and *bayaderes* – sacred dancers who serve in the temple - live in the area on this side of the photograph that forms part of the pagoda. Travelers are also welcome inside the "refuge" that can house as many as a thousand people.

AND OFF IN THE DISTANCE IN THIS FLAT LAND [...] SOMETHING UNIQUE AND DISCONCERTING CATCHES THE EYE: it looks like a large golden bell crowned by a golden handle ... It is gold without a doubt, for it shines with too delicate a luster to be anything else. [...] It is [...] the most holy pagoda in all of Burma containing the relics of the five Buddhas and the three horses of Gautama [...]. It is a 1000 years old; since ancient times the faithful have flocked here from the four corners of Asia, laden with gold and treasures, especially gold, gold plate and gold leaf, to add to that magnificent layer of gilt on the great tower twinkling in the distance in the sun. And for centuries, the pagoda has shone that in that fashion, never changing.

Pierre Loti, 1909

Left: the typically Burmese bell-shaped *stupa*, associated since the 11th century with Pagan and Mandalay. The Great Pagoda of Rangoon (right) was built according to legend 600 years before the present era and was renovated in the 18th century by Alompra, founder of the last Burmese dynasty.
Inset: Strand Hotel baggage label.

Following double-page display: the King of Siam's automobile and hundreds of passers-by in the main thoroughfare of Bangkok c. 1910, an astonishing sight for a town with such a water-borne image . . . . At the time, the capital of Thailand, washed by the waters of the Menang river and crowded with junks and houses on stilts, was a busy port despite the sandbank. Rama V who ruled there until 1910, had in truth traveled widely in Europe and the Siamese had sent an ambassador to Versailles as early as 1684: travel was by no means one-way.

THE PRESENT CAPITAL IS ONLY 100 YEARS OLD but already grown to 10 miles in circumference and is inhabited by more than 500,000 people. [...] With its countless canals, it is the Venice of Asia, magnificently colorful with its peeling roofs and luminous mosaics and strangely picturesque with its thousands of boats that sail between the greenery and the multicolored pagodas. In the midst of these rafts and floating houses it is impossible to tell, where terra firma begins and ends.

Paul Bonnetain, 1887

At the beginning of 1888 Joseph Conrad was in Bangkok, waiting to assume his first command, a small three-master called the *Otago*. He spent a fortnight in the brand new Continental Hotel where he stayed in Room No. 1, now called the "Conrad Suite," overlooking the river. By this time the old Oriental, pictured on the right c. 1910, was merely the "writers' wing" of the new hotel. From one of the windows above the steps, Conrad would have had a view over the river and could imagine the China Sea beyond.

Left: old photographs celebrating the Oriental Hotel in its heyday feature (bottom) Prince Valdemar of Denmark and his retinue on the deck of the royal yacht during a visit to Bangkok in 1900; (center) presentation of a new model of automobile in the grounds of the Oriental in 1929.

Following double-page display:
The King of Siam's elephants. "Elephants are caught using beaters who chase them into the pens. Next, domesticated elephants are let into the pens who soon calm the new arrivals and help to make them less wild," explains the 1930s edition of the *Grand Larousse*. Scots tourists visiting the sawmill of MacGregor & Co., just outside Rangoon, saw a team of nine elephants with perfectly coordinated movements who would even close one eye every now and then to check a measurement. When they broke for lunch from 12 noon to 3.00 pm no-one would ever have dreamed of disturbing them . . . .

S 14. Saïgon

SAïGON
HOTEL MAJESTIC

SHE HAD DIFFICULTY IMAGINING HIM IN REAL LIFE, the way he might be this Saturday night in his bedroom at the Hôtel Majestic, looking out of the window beyond the Rue Catinat to the bend in the river Saigon that headed off through the Cochin- Chinese countryside. He could imagine the wharves, picture the masts and funnels of the ships of the *Messageries Maritimes*. In the middle of the river, surrounded by sampans sailing back and forth, were two freighters hanging on their chains.

Edouard Lavergne, 1941

Saigon's impressive post office building (above), just before the Officers' Club, was at the top of the Rue Catinat, the main thoroughfare that started at the confluence of the river Saigon and the Chinatown Creek. It was lined with tamarind trees and was not surfaced until the 1920s. The post office was opposite the cathedral and the famous Hôtel Continental with its terrace resonant with the pulse of the colony.
Inset: baggage label of the Hôtel

Majestic, another of Saigon's grand hotels.
Images of the capital of Indochina c. 1900 (right) that the writer Malraux recalls in the following terms in his *Antimémoires*:
"The boredom of Cochin China, the pith helmets, the leafy hour on the terrace of the Continental when the short night fell on the carob trees and the victorias crossing in the Rue Catinat with their bells jingling, and the lights going out in the barracks of the

Senegalese infantry . . . ."
From top to bottom: the symbolic tiger on a brochure for the Continental; view of a road in Cholon (the Chinese quarter of Saigon); Europeans in colonial whites on board the *Tourane* in 1907 (page from a photograph album). The ship was named after the town of Tourane – or Da Nang – the first town captured by the French in 1858.

CONTINENTAL
PALACE

Cochinchine

a bord
"douman"

à Chợ Lớn

THERE WERE GALLERIES EVERYWHERE, AND STAIRWAYS AS STEEP AS LADDERS with high, narrow steps. The Khmers must have been long-legged men who never suffered from vertigo. I have been up dozens of those stairs and speak from painful experience. To say nothing of the descent which was even worse than the climb.

C. W. Leadbeater, 1929

Lianas clinging to the faces of the divinities at the temple of Bayon (above) and a shaven-haired monk in bright yellow robes who symbolizes oriental wisdom. The late 12th- and early 13th-century mountainous temple of Bayon, located in the center of the enclosure of Angkor Thorm, was one of the last flowerings of Khmer art: *devatas* (goddesses) and *apsaras* (celestial female dancers) wore necklaces that passed between the breasts and round the waist, triangular-shaped tiaras and narrow scarves that floated around their waists like ribbons. In 1860, when the explorer Henri Mouhot asked his guides who had built these temples, they replied "the *apsaras*" and showed him the marks left by their celestial fingers on blocks of sandstone that they had brought with them from Indra's paradise.

Right: beautifully chiseled they may have been, beautifully fitted they were not . . . unless of course they were intended to collapse under the feet of bellicose invaders Following double-page display: the temple of Bayon as it today.

THE EASTERN AND ORIENTAL ONLY REALLY BECAME a grand hotel when it was taken over by the younger of the Sarkies brothers, Arshak. Everyone worshipped Arshak, from the bellhop to royalty and millionaires staying in the hotel. In the 1920s, the new owner spared no expense. Nothing was too good: parties, evening dances to the rhythm of the foxtrot, fireworks that lit up the entire seafront. Arshak was also extremely tolerant of people who left without paying their bills.

Catherine Donzel, 1985

Built in 1922, the Victory Annex and its domes (left) were linked a year later to the main building of the Eastern & Oriental in George Town by a gigantic ballroom. The hotel's frontage on the sea was now nearly 920 feet long.
Right: the funicular railway that runs from the Botanical Gardens up through screeching monkeys to the top of Penang Hill, at an altitude of 2,300 feet. Halfway up is the "temple of serpents that all the lady passengers talk about and swear never to visit but that each of them visits all the same," wrote Roland Dorgelès.

At the top of Penang Hill is the Crag Hotel (above in 1990, and below c. 1930) built in 1891. Like the Eastern & Oriental it was part of the Sarkies brothers' empire and consisted of two- or three-roomed family bungalows. The smaller photographs below show a general view of the hill – taken from the same angle as the more recent photo above – plus the main hotel building and the driveway leading up to it. Day turns seamlessly to night in the tropics, usually at about 6.00 pm, whatever the season. From the top of Penang Hill, however, there is magnificent view all day of the island and its port where the big ships drop anchor.

MIDNIGHT. The last houses and last lights in Singapore have disappeared behind a fold in the landscape; this is the heart of the countryside, thick with greenery. The powerful, tangled vegetation commences at the very doors of the city and covers the entire peninsula. [...] Palm trees of every conceivable shape that shine in the moonlight like sheet metal; [...] And strangest of all, the *traveler's trees* with their large, beautifully symmetrical leaves that fan out like a peacock's tail, resembling immense Chinese screens growing in the woods.

Pierre Loti, 1883

Englishmen in dinner jackets, shiny dance floor and that table decorated with orchids where Chinese waiters in white served us curry. "One degree from the equator," I repeated to myself, sticking my fork into those little dishes full of mango peel, grated coconut, red fish from Macassar and goodness knows what else they add to the rice that sets your mouth on fire as you swallow it. "One degree from the equator" and the ladies ask for their shawls because it is too cold beneath the fans . . . ." (Roland Dorgelès, *Partir ...*)

On this floor of the hotel, all the suites overlook the Palm Garden, called the *Palm Court*. Guests can relax on the gallery with the sounds of the grand hotel wafting up from below. The prolific vegetation creeps into the very depths of the building and the air is so humid that any room remaining closed for three days will be covered in mold. In the scullery, shoes are polished with hibiscus flowers or mangosteen peel and knives are polished with pineapple juice.

The docks in Tanjong Pagar, two miles from Singapore, where once the Mail ships arrived (above, c. 1890). Right: the so-called "traveler's tree" (photo dating from the 1890s) whose leaves quite literally radiate like an outstretched fan: new leaves grow from the center as the lowest leaves on either side wither and die.
The legendary Raffles Hotel in Singapore (following double-page display) offers travelers protection from the climate just as the Embassy protects them from awkward situations. "I definitely plan to see the Raffles again, with its orchestra and cocktails,

THERE IS A HOTEL IN SINGAPORE — the city where you can sit and watch the ships of all the world go by. That means steamers and freighters, yachts and white winged sailing ships, and junks, and myriads of tiny paddling craft that fret the water with their ceaseless motion. You can sit at your table and see all this if you face the right way, for the sea swims off blue through all the white doors and openings.

Atlantic Monthly Magazine, c. 1910

SINGAPORE

Left: Raffles archive material; a letter written by an English guest typical of those who haunted the mythical hotel. Having boarded the steamer in Brindisi, he is now in Singapore from where he will go to Calcutta, Bombay and Rome. Mail can reach him "care of Thos. Cook." The hotel archives are full of such letters, not to mention the Guest Book bearing such illustrious signatures as those of Kipling, Maugham, Conrad and all the great writers or travelers who stayed at the Raffles. It is named after Sir Stamford Raffles, born off the coast of Jamaica, who was appointed first governor of the Dutch East Indies and then — once he had persuaded his government to acquire it - Malaya. What better emblem for a grand hotel . . . .

The Sarkies brothers were not wrong to make the Raffles the flagship hotel of an empire that included the Eastern & Oriental, the Crag, the Raffles-by-the-Sea of Penang and two hotels in Surabaya run by another branch of the family.
Above: the murmuring of the equatorial jungle in the Raffles gardens, bathed in the perfumed torpor of the blue night.

BATAVIA IS THE KIND OF TOWN THAT ONLY EXISTS IN FAIRY TALES [...] The river is policed by the crocodiles that infest its waters. [...] But where, you ask, is the town? Right here! Notice the big roads and little lanes winding through the thick forest. The houses meanwhile, tucked away in thickets, surrounded by gardens and bathed in shadow, are barely visible. All the houses look alike. They are one story high (rarely two) with a large veranda that projects out from the corners of the façade into the front garden — usually a flowerbed surrounded by railings and decorated with statuettes and vases.

Count Joseph von Hübner, 1886

The Hôtel des Indes in Batavia in 1903 (above). Outside the main building wait the two carriages needed to transport a pair of travelers. Naturally the larger of the two, the cart, is for the impressive quantity of luggage including some hefty-looking steamer trunks. The old town of Batavia, dating from the early 18th century, was full of red brick houses with steep stoops like those in Amsterdam. These passers-by (right), standing stiffly beneath the trees, do seem to be the worthy descendants of the austere colonials who sailed here with the East India Company. Insert: 1934 *Monterey* passenger manifest.

Following double-page display: Borobodur, the great wonder of Java. Walls a mile and a half long carved with bas-reliefs illustrate the life of Prince Siddhartha Gautama and how he became the Buddha after discovering the four Holy Truths. The carvings display all of the flora and fauna of Java: its culture, finery, musical instruments and the entire pantheon of Mahayana Buddhism including some delightful fairies. On the outskirts of the temple, before entering the forest (previous double-page display), the ground is carpeted with sensitive plants that fold their leaves as visitors approach and open them again once the danger has passed. The sight is enough to stop anybody in their tracks . . . .

Russia

St. Petersburg

Moscow

Kazak

Poland

Germany

Boston
New York

Paris

France

Marseilles

Italy

Genoa

Spain

Portugal

Turkey

Gibraltar

Tunisia

Syria

Moroccco

Port-Said

Iraq

Alexandria

Algeria

Suez

Lybia

Egypt

Saudi Arabia

Oman

Eritrea

Yemen

Sudan

Somalia

Ethiopia

From Paris to Peking
on the Trans-Siberian

From Singapore to Hong Kong
with the *Messageries Maritimes*

From Boston to Kobe with
the Dollar Steamship Line

From San Francisco to Yokohama
with the Pacific Steamship
Company

Sites

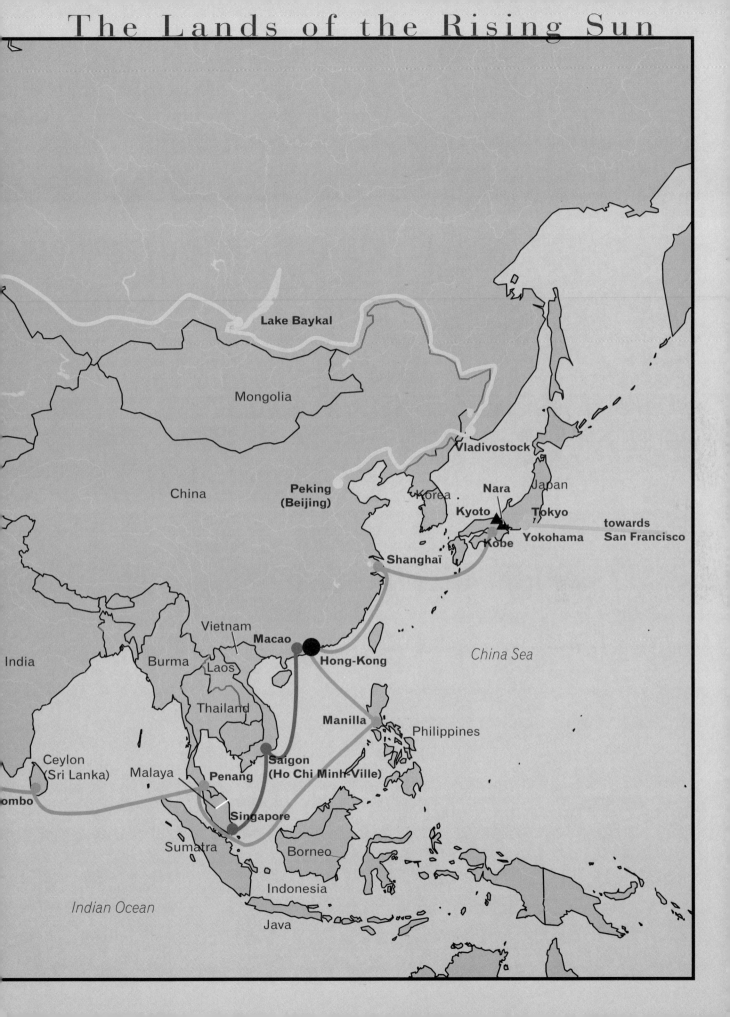

The Lands of the Rising Sun

Lake Baykal

Mongolia

China

Vladivostock

**Peking
(Beijing)**

Korea

Japan

Nara

Kyoto

Tokyo

Kobe

Yokohama

**towards
San Francisco**

Shanghaï

Vietnam

Macao

India

Burma

Laos

Hong-Kong

China Sea

Thailand

Manilla

Philippines

Ceylon
(Sri Lanka)

Malaya

Penang

**Saigon
(Ho Chi Minh-Ville)**

ombo

Singapore

Sumatra

Borneo

Indonesia

Indian Ocean

Java

The Trans-Siberian, as its name suggests, was one of those trains "in transit." Siberia was not a place you visited, strictly a place you passed through. Trains crossed continents the way ships crossed the waters. They were ships on dry land and this one traveled to the Lands of the Rising Sun, to Japan and China, linking Western Europe with the Pacific, Paris and Petrograd with Vladivostock. It took just two weeks by train from Paris to Peking by way of Irkutsk compared with at least a month by boat from

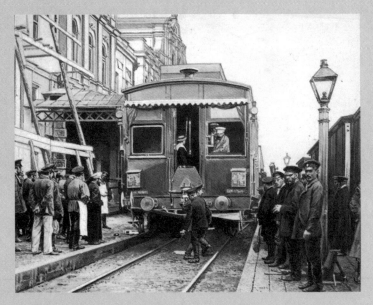

Marseilles to Shanghai. It was a poetic journey, one undertaken by the poet Blaise Cendrars "forever caught between meridians." It was an elitist journey, affordable for barely 1,500 Europeans a year before the Bolshevik revolution. ❦ The Trans-Siberian beat every record: more than 6,000 miles of track through 250 stations including Omsk, Krasnoyarsk, Tomsk, Irkutsk, Harbin, and Mukden, eventually reaching the labyrinthine city of Peking with its concentric walls, Chinese City, Tartar City, Yellow City, Red City, Temple of Heaven and Coal Hill, Marble Bridge …. ❦ In 1928 Peking ceded its title as capital to Nanking but Shanghai "the wealthy" remained China's banking center and the place where all the great political intrigues were hatched. The Chinese Communist Party held its first congress on French property. And in the adjoining building of the Cathay Hôtel — where journalist Albert Londres was known to stay — the conspirators, protected by the privilege of foreign status, plotted Mao's takeover. French mail went from Shanghai to Paris at French postal rates on the Trans-Siberian. In Zi-Ka-wei meanwhile, the Jesuit mission kept well out of politics and devoted itself to study, science and the formation of an elite. ❦ Saigon was the second home port of the *Messageries Maritimes* after Marseilles, with boats leaving for Haiphong, Hong Kong and Shanghai and sailing gently down the Mekong to the mouth of the river some 60 miles away. It is said that the Portuguese

national poet Camoëns was shipwrecked on his return from Macao when he was carrying the manuscript of *The Lusiads* — the great epic tale of the exploits of Vasco de Gama and his companions. Camoëns apparently saved the manuscript from a watery grave by holding it at arms' length above his head... ❦ Macao, three days away by sea, is a peninsula in the shape of an amphitheater. "Macao, *L'Enfer du Jeu*." Four centuries after Camoëns nearly drowned there, the town gave its name to a card game that was one of

the many variants of 21 (Macao or "Nine"). ⦃ Hong-Kong opposite, together with Singapore and Shanghai, was one of the three great western trading posts in the East. Fortunes changed hands there with the unfailing regularity of propeller blades cutting the water. Shanghai could also be reached from the Atlantic coast of America, from Boston or New York via Gibraltar, Suez and Colombo. On the way, you would cross the American archipelago of the Philippines studded with 7,000 islets and islands, some with volcanoes spewing fire others, like Jolo, surrounded by seas laden with pearls and nacre. ⦃ From Shanghai to Kobe was a four-day journey across the Inland Sea. Kobe was merely the port for Osaka, the Empire's chief commercial city. The spirit of the "Land of the Rising Sun" lay in Kyoto, where between the Mikado's Palace and the Shogun's fortress visitors could buy Eirakou porcelain with golden designs on a red background. ⦃ Passengers arriving from the Pacific coast and San Francisco landed directly at Yokohama like the officer in *Madame Butterfly*. And there was Tokyo, with its temples and tombs, magnificent parks and hills of Shiba and Ueno. And Yoshiwara, the city that never slept. Here at the beginning of April, tubs of cherry trees were placed along the Nakanocho, the main avenue where the courtesans tittuped barefoot on their high, black-lacquered *geta* (clogs). They lived in the *Kado Tamaya* (House of the Peonies), the *Matsubaya* (House of the Peacock) or the *Ebiya* (House of the Phoenix). They wore the traditional *obi*, a wide silk belt that tied in a bow at the front and their hair was studded with tortoiseshell combs. Behind them came their *shinzos* (apprentices) and their *kamuros*, young girls whose hair was patterned with flowers and held in place by silken cords.

Alain Rustenholz

Above: postcard of the Pacific Mail Steamship & Co. on sale to passengers sailing to China on the *S.S. Manchuria* c. 1880. Left: 1930s label of the Cathay and Metropole Hotels in Shanghai. Right: dinner menu for *Empress of Britain* passengers on 8 March 1933, offered by the Hotel New Grand of Yokohama. Previous pages: the smiling stewards of the Peninsula, Hong Kong's last historic grand hotel (p.224); smokers' platform on the Trans-Siberian (p. 225 above) and interior of lounge carriage on the Trans-Manchurian in 1923 (p. 225 below). Insert: former currency of the Banca Nacional Ultramarino, the national Portuguese bank of Macao before the town reverted to Chinese rule.

WELCOME DINNER DANCE

FOR THE

"Empress of Britain"

MENU

Clear Soup in Cup

Cold Salmon Mayonnaise Sauce

Supreme of Chicken with Rice

French Beans in Butter

Roast Beef with Rissole Potatoes

Salad in Season

Coupe Praline

Fruits

Coffee

Wed. March 8th. 1933

HOTEL NEW GRAND

YOKOHAMA

Macao! that gloomy, sad and silent town... A condemned city, ravaged by typhoons and left desolate amid the ruins by men who are even more cruel! Stranger than anything I have ever visited, it looms up all of a sudden, with its silent streets where the only noise is my echoing footsteps, its deserted port caked in mud and its ugly ruins a testament to its past prosperity and defunct glory ...

Paul Bonnetain, 1887

MACAO

As traditional as ever, the ancient teahouse of Loe Koe (above), moments away from the casinos that every weekend attract thousands of gamblers from China. Here, far from the rowdy, frenetic atmosphere of the roulette tables and the blackjack players, Chinese from Macao come to drink their tea just as they did 100 years ago.
Macao, the first western bridgehead on the borders of China in the 16th century, ceased being a Portuguese province in December 1999 when it reverted to Chinese rule.
Right: a terrace of the Hotel Bela Vista overlooking the bay of the goddess Ama – "Amacao" from whence comes "Macao" in Portuguese – at the mouth of the "River of Pearls." Shrouded in mist across the bay is the outline of the modern town, immortalized in the film L'enfer du Jeu.

THE LANDING FORMALITIES IN MACAO WERE PRACTICALLY NONEXISTENT. I left what little luggage I had with the coolie and set off to explore the wharves. Everything in that port was on a delightfully small scale - pontoons, warehouses, customs house, boats, workshops – everything but for the sea of junks that spread out in a long line, side by side, as far as the eye could see. "There are 9,000 of them in Macao alone, not to mention the surrounding area," comments someone in English suddenly, right by my ear. [...] "My name is Manoel and I am a genuine Portuguese man from Macao, which means that I have a great deal of Chinese blood in me [he smiles], as you can see."

Joseph Kessel, 1957

The Bela Vista was founded around 1870 by an English couple, Captain Clarke and his wife Catherine Hannack, who originally called it the "Boa Vista Hotel." In 1901, after being sold to the French government of Indochina, who converted it to a military hospital, the hotel was bought back by the Portuguese who turned it into a charitable institution, then a school, a post office headquarters and an asylum center for Portuguese refugees from northern China. Not until 1947 did it come to be a hotel again under the name of Bela Vista – but not for long. When Macao returned to the bosom of the People's Republic of China, the Bela Vista became a consulate.

And yet in the late 19th century this was one of the finest hotels in the Far East. At the time these photographs were taken, the Bela Vista possessed an old-fashioned charm that was absent from other such establishments.

Following double-page display: the garish colors of a makeshift altar on the streets of Macao for Chinese New Year. Fake money (known as "Hell's Banknotes") is traditionally burnt as an offering.

STANDING AT THE VERY PEAK OF THE ISLAND, a single glance can encompass the bays and the creeks, the roofs and the flowers, the red, washed-out roads, the undulating green slopes and the yellow ochre hilltop villages, with the immense city laid out below, descending in tiers from street to street to the surface of the waters, while across the arm of the sea stretches the glimmering outline of another city that is more enormous still [...]. Then, lost in contemplation, dazzled and exhilarated, you feel a strange and wonderful fear well up from the depths of your enchantment.

Joseph Kessel, 1957

Rickshaws and palanquins circulate in the steep streets of Hong Kong (above), between the outrageous garlands of crimson morning glory that scramble right to the tops of the houses. All around the city, the high retaining walls that hold back the earth are crowned with rows of potted plants, the ground being too stony to dig gardens.

The Peninsula Hotel, designed by architects Palmer & Turner, was triumphantly inaugurated in 1928 after a four-year delay due to the presence of occupying British troops (which incidentally, was just a foretaste of the Japanese occupation in 1943). The gigantic building towers over Kowloon Peninsula, Hong Kong's scrap of continental coast. In the north of the island is the capital Victoria, in the south is the port of Aberdeen and between the two are banana trees.

Below: Peninsula Hotel baggage label.

Right: A view of the Bay of Hong Kong in the 1980s from Victoria Peak. People who know the island these days are surprised at how much it has changed in the past 20 years …

Following double-page display: view of Hong Kong in 1904 with not a skyscraper in sight. The funicular (in the foreground) climbed valiantly up the steep flanks of Victoria Peak to an altitude of 1,600 feet. From there, the big three-masters anchored in the bay (visible on the right) with their decks covered with tarpaulins look like marquees surrounded by sea.

234

WHAT A WONDERFUL SURPRISE WHEN YOU LAND ON THE BUND, otherwise known as the concessionary wharf. Elegant houses - or should I say palaces — on either side, some surrounded by greenery, each one grander than the next. [...] The *Bund* at close of business when businessmen are once again gentlemen is a sight to behold. There are as many black suits as Chinese plaits at the entrance to the English Club, and any newcomer seeing the fashionable outfits of the European ladies setting off for their walk to the Bubbling Well might almost think he was back in the Champs Elysées or Hyde Park.

Paul Bonnetain, 1887

The international concessionary wharf in Shanghai in 1900 (left) known as the *Bund* – or in the case of the French concession, the "Quai de France" – home of the celebrated Shanghai Club and the British and American consulates. On the corner of the Bund, on the left of the photo, is the Central, the oldest hotel in Shanghai, built in 1870 and later enlarged to accommodate a further 120 bedrooms and renamed the "Palace Hotel." This is where journalist Albert Londres stayed in 1932, on his last assignment to Shanghai. The Palace subsequently merged with the Cathay to form the Peace Hotel, the oldest of the existing grand hotels in Shanghai.

Right: a junk all decked out for the ceremony of the Dragon in Shanghai Bay in 1907. At the end of the 1920s, the Chinese government did away with the old calendar but "New Year" remained as the "Spring Festival." This was not just any calendar date but the moment when the god of the home rose up to the Heavens to tell Chang-Ti, the Lord on High, about everything that had happened in the house in the course of the year. Following double-page display: the plaits that to a tourist seem so characteristic of the Chinese were in fact a discriminatory measure forced upon them in 1645 by the Manchu conquerors. The sight of this train in China recalls Albert Londres' description of himself when he stayed there for the first time in 1922: "He traveled as others might smoke opium or sniff coke. It was his particular vice. He got high on sleeping cars and steamships. And after years of useless trips around the world he could safely say that neither a look from an intelligent woman, who was not bad at that, nor the entire contents of a safe, held the same diabolical fascination for him as a small, rectangular train ticket."

IN THE CHINSE CITY [of Peking] where all of the commercial and industrial activity seems to be concentrated, there are entire streets of shops with an excellent stock of native goods and a few European items. Pharmacies, teashops and tobacco stores can be distinguished by their magnificent gold and lacquer frontages and by the huge vertical signs that hang from poles outside the door.

Count Joseph von Hübner, 1886

These two superb photographs dating from 1928 convey the image of a country with a thousand faces and a multitude of peoples.
Left: the Great Wall of China. This crenellated wall that stretches for 1,875 miles was begun in the 3rd century B.C. to keep out the Huns, and it remains the most enduring symbol of the Empire's resistance to outside influences. China, world center of civilization, had nothing to learn from the barbarians. Until the end of the Ming Dynasty in 1644, overseas trade was punishable by death and the country remained officially closed under the Manchu (Qin) Dynasty.
Right: the Doung-Bien-Men belfry has "that solidity, that massiveness that we Westerners associate with the idea of power. None of the buildings is built to last because the idea of "investing in stone" does not exist. Indeed, over the centuries, everything - palaces, temples, houses – has been rebuilt on the same model."
(*La Chine*, Larousse)

Peking (Beijing) capital of northern China, capital of all of China, was "much more than a city, a symbol of imperial power and of the pivotal position it held between the Earth, Mankind and the Heavens." Peking, intellectual capital where men of letters have fought a constant battle against obscurantism and where the western presence has not always been welcome . . . .

Above: two views of the interior of the Grand Hôtel de Pékin in 1920, three years after it was rebuilt: the vast entrance hall (left) opens onto a lounge furnished with rattan that included a boutique in the corner selling cameras and Kodak film.

The first Grand Hôtel, built in 1900, came under fire in the Boxer Rebellion against foreign interests in China. Subsequently, in the troubles of 1922, Albert Londres who was staying at the hotel received the following advice from his interpreter who was hoping to seek refuge there: "You are staying at the Hôtel de Pékin – the best hotel of all. You should move out however. Just think where the hotel is. Right in the thick of things! A haven for bloodthirsty cutthroats. You should take your bags to the Hôtel des Wagons-Lits, in the Legation Quarter. The Quarter is surrounded by walls and above all it enjoys the privileges of extra-

territoriality." Albert Londres did not move but Mr Pou sought cover in his bedroom, No 518, all the same.
Insets: postcard and baggage label of the Grand Hotel de Pékin.

In a word, Peking is a rectangle resembling one of those boxes that you find on sale in bazaars, boxes that contain boxes inside boxes. It is surrounded by 22 to 33 miles of feudal fortifications and occupies a trifling 15,664 acres, which is equal to four-fifths of the area of Paris!

Paul Bonnetain, 1887

JUST WHERE THE UNSUSPECTING HAD HOPED TO FIND DOLL'S HOUSES, PAPER HOUSES AND WOMEN IN KIMONOS, they bump into longshoremen and dockyard workers with gas masks over their mouths and noses: Yokohama is a not an appealing sight to lovers of the picturesque. However the harbor of this major commercial port does look lovely, especially when seen from the Foreigners' Cemetery.

Paul Mousset, 1956

Right: Yokohama, c. 1880. Behind the cavorting sailors and the junks lies the Bund: the embankment quay on the seafront with its hotels, clubs, offices and private houses, all in the European style. Residential villas with big gardens planted with trees are stepped up the hillside overlooking the bay, beyond the very flat coastal strip. Inset: baggage label of the Imperial Hotel in Tokyo, a remarkable building designed by Frank Lloyd Wright that survived the earthquake of 1923 but not the property fever of 1968, when it was demolished.
Left: in this universe full of symbolic meaning, flowers in the hair suggest an apprentice courtesan.
Following double-page display: the newspaper rack of the New Grand Hotel in Yokohama in 1985. Passengers arriving from Vancouver were always desperate for news after 12 days at sea without a break on one of those P & O ships that turn around and go back again every three weeks.
Previous double-page display: drooping clusters of wisteria in the Kameido district of Tokyo, a gridwork of canals and bridges on the eastern bank of the river Sumida. The area is famous for its gardens of plum trees, Tenjin Sanctuary and the etching artist Kunisada, who used to live opposite. Temples usually rent part of their land to restaurants and pleasure houses, so it anybody's guess where these passers-by might be headed ...

How uneven, changeable and strange Kyoto is! Streets that remain noisy, cluttered with *gaijin* (foreigners), pedestrians, merchants, garish posters and extravagant banners that flutter in the wind. One moment a frenzy of noise and cries; the next the silence of abandoned things, the debris of a great dead past. Surrounded by glittering displays of fabrics and porcelain; or approaching the grand temples with the idol sellers opening their stores filled with unimaginable figures; or even suddenly surprised to find yourself in a forest of bamboo beneath tightly packed spears of amazingly tall reedy canes …Kyoto, that gigantic sanctuary of worship of former Emperors is an immense religious shambles!

Pierre Loti, 1889

KYOTO

Kyoto succeeded Nara as the imperial capital, which Nara had been for 11 centuries. It is built on the Chinese T'ang Dynasty model of a capital that positioned temples away from the life of the city. It was to escape their hold that the Mikado had just abandoned Nara. Above: the "upside-down" bridge of Sanjo, in Kyoto, for walks or meditation.
Right: the late 16th- to early 17th-century temple of Hongan-ji, built by the warlord Hideyoshi who attempted to conquer China. Hence the pronounced Chinese influence of the door design.
Inset: Kyoto Hotel baggage label.

Following double-page display: the bell of the temple of Daibutsu, in Nara. The bronze Daibutsu (or Great Buddha) of Nara is the most ancient of the colossal statues of the Buddha. It was erected in 749 A.D., during the time when the imperial capital of Nara was the focus of the Chinese Buddhist influence from Korea that would spread throughout the archipelago. The largest bell in Japan, one of the biggest in the world, is in Kyoto. It weighs 78 tons and measures one foot in thickness.

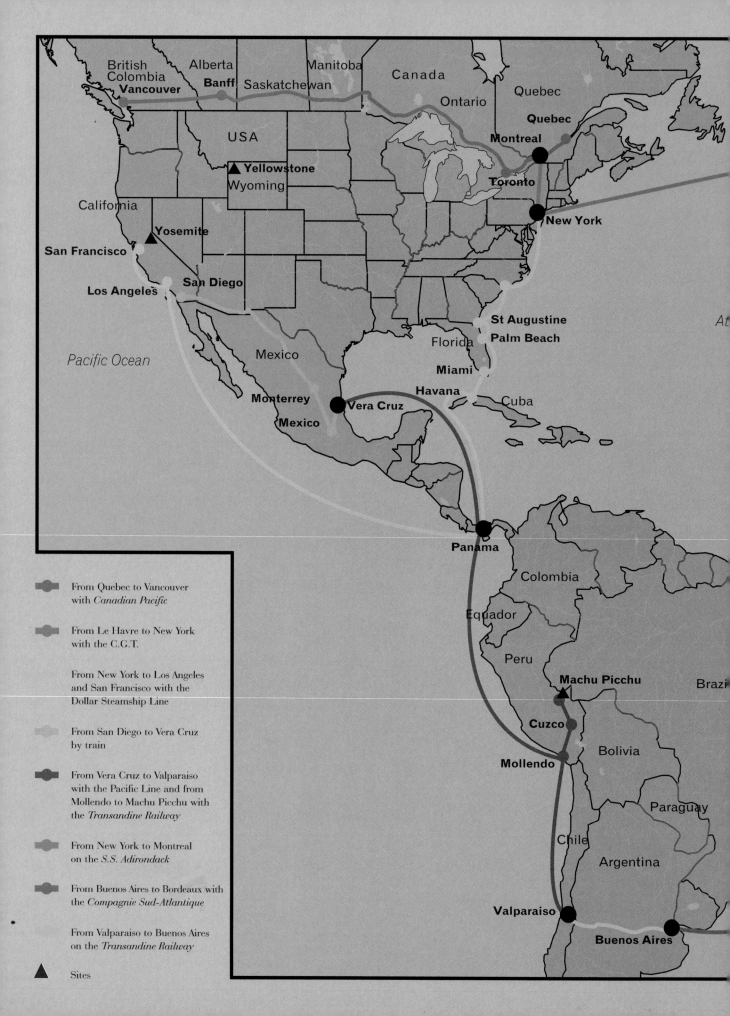

British
Colombia
Vancouver
Banff
Alberta
Saskatchewan
Manitoba
Canada
Ontario
Quebec
Quebec
Montreal
Toronto
New York

USA
▲ **Yellowstone**
Wyoming

California
▲ **Yosemite**
San Francisco
Los Angeles
San Diego

Pacific Ocean

St Augustine
Palm Beach
Florida
Miami
Havana
Cuba

At

Mexico
Monterrey
Mexico
Vera Cruz

Panama

Colombia

Equador

Peru

Machu Picchu ▲
Brazi

Cuzco
Bolivia

Mollendo

Paraguay

Chile

Argentina

Valparaiso

Buenos Aires

From Quebec to Vancouver
with *Canadian Pacific*

From Le Havre to New York
with the C.G.T.

From New York to Los Angeles
and San Francisco with the
Dollar Steamship Line

From San Diego to Vera Cruz
by train

From Vera Cruz to Valparaiso
with the Pacific Line and from
Mollendo to Machu Picchu with
the *Transandine Railway*

From New York to Montreal
on the *S.S. Adirondack*

From Buenos Aires to Bordeaux with
the *Compagnie Sud-Atlantique*

From Valparaiso to Buenos Aires
on the *Transandine Railway*

▲ Sites

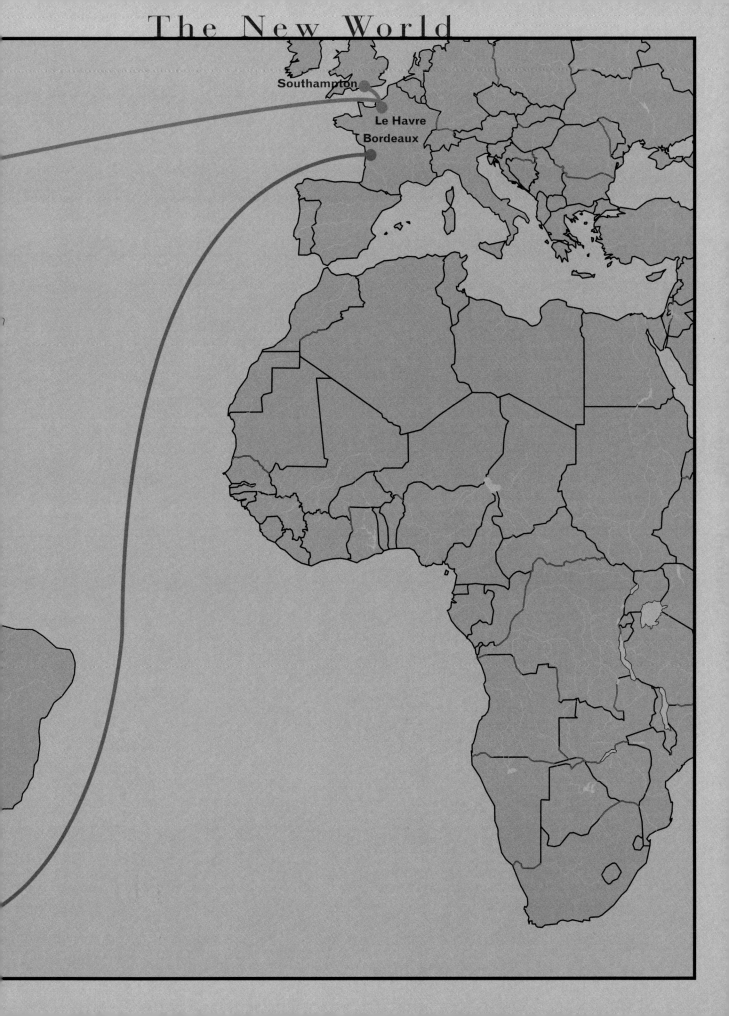

Southampton

Le Havre
Bordeaux

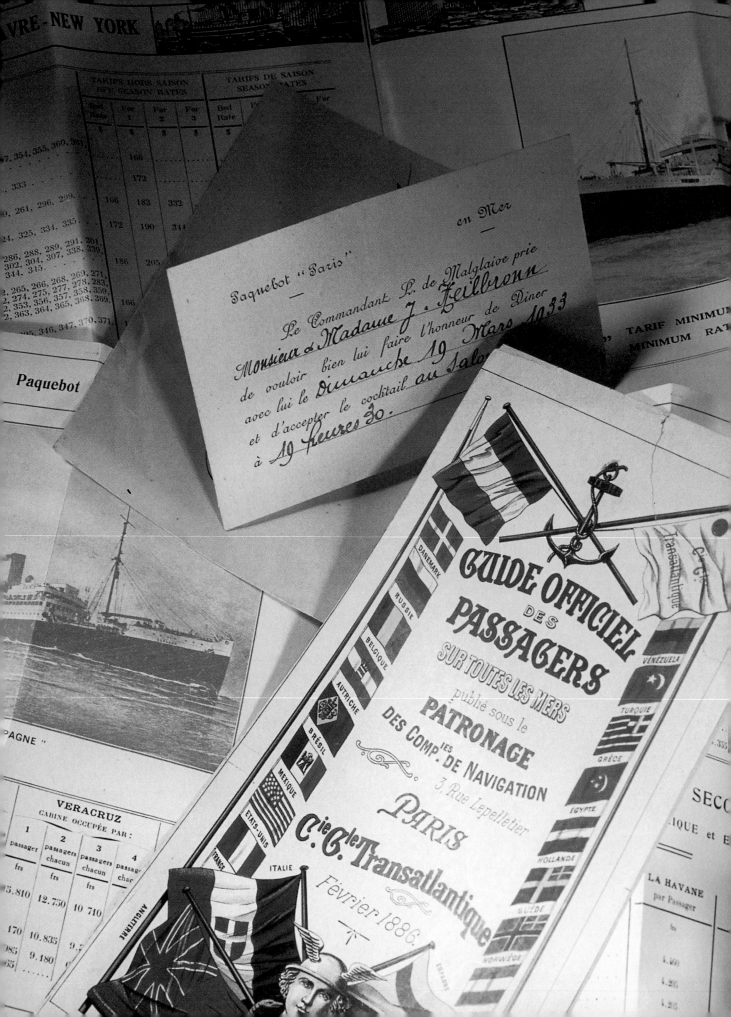

HAVRE-NEW YORK

	TARIFS HORS SAISON OFF SEASON RATES			TARIFS DE SAISON SEASON RATES		
	Bed Rate $	For 2 $	For 3 $	Bed Rate $	For 2 $	For 3 $
7, 354, 355, 360, 361		166				
. 333		172				
9, 261, 296, 299		166	183	332		
24, 325, 334, 335		172	190	314		
286, 288, 289, 291, 301, 302, 304, 307		186	205			
344, 315						
2, 265, 266, 268, 269, 271, 2, 353, 356, 357, 358, 359, 2, 363, 364, 365, 368, 369		166				

Paquebot

Paquebot "Paris"   en Mer

Le Commandant P. de Malglaive prie
Monsieur & Madame J. Feilbrenn
de vouloir bien lui faire l'honneur de Diner
avec lui le Dimanche 19 Mars 1933
et d'accepter le cocktail au Salon
à 19 heures 30.

"PARIS" TARIF MINIMUM
MINIMUM RAT

GUIDE OFFICIEL DES PASSAGERS SUR TOUTES LES MERS
publié sous le
PATRONAGE
des Comp. DE NAVIGATION
3, Rue Lepelletier
PARIS
C.ie G.le Transatlantique
Février 1886.

DANEMARK — RUSSIE — BELGIQUE — AUTRICHE — BRÉSIL — MEXIQUE — ÉTATS-UNIS — FRANCE — ITALIE — VÉNÉZUELA — TURQUIE — GRÈCE — ÉGYPTE — HOLLANDE — SUÈDE — NORWÉGE

SEC
LIQUE et

VERACRUZ CABINE OCCUPÉE PAR :			
1 passager frs	2 passagers chacun frs	3 passagers chacun frs	4 passage chac frs
5.810	12.750	10 710	
170	10.835	9.	
985	9.180		

LA HAVANE
par Passager
frs

AGNE "

In colonial times, ships to the Orient carried large numbers of civil servants, the military, missionaries and other passengers who were toughened by the punishing overseas climate and rarely making the journey for the first time. The Atlantic crossing was something else altogether. Picasso's "Demoiselles d'Avignon" sailed on board the *Normandie*, as did all of the most famous Hollywood stars. In Paris meanwhile, Simone de Beauvoir waited at the Gare Saint Lazare to meet her American lover Nelson Algren, off the transatlantic train. ❦ The scale was not the same either: with 2,000 passengers on board, the *Normandie* carried five times as many passengers as the *Champollion*, sailing in Mediterranean waters. For people going to New York, the sea crossing was an unpleasant necessity and not something to be enjoyed. Companies were endlessly vying with each

other to make the journey faster and shorter. The sea was frightening. Even at the height of summer, the foghorn could sound all night, making sleep impossible. Occasionally the crew would inform passengers that at 2.30 in the morning the ship had met with one of those icebergs the size of castles that floated southward at that time of year. The only solution was to pile on the luxury and the entertainment, which every shipping company did with a vengeance. The gay social whirl continued non-stop for four days, three hours and two minutes. The *Normandie* and later the *France* became famous as the "Champs-Elysées-on-the Sea" and other fashionable districts in Paris. Luxury was not just something expected by VIPs: it was a tranquilizer. There was simply no point in going up on deck — too bad if you missed seeing a whale near the Grand Bank, off the Newfoundland coast. In any case, it took far too long to regroup a long row of deckchairs in little circles: breaking the ice was much quicker in the bar! ❦ For passengers from New York who had traveled northward by train on the *Adirondack*, the sophistication of life on board ship was in sharp contrast to the frozen wastes, primeval rocks and vegetation of the journey up into Canada. There was Quebec with its 17th-century citadel that centuries later became a hotel; there was Montreal, that little corner of history, Europe,

Cunard EUROPE UNITED STATES CANADA — Through bookings to and from all parts of the world. Offices and agencies everywhere

faith and classical architecture in modern America; then the rest was nothing but trees. Trees felled and stacked outside the immense sawmills of Ottawa ready to be made into sidewalks in towns that sprang up overnight. Trees growing in gigantic forests of ubiquitous maple that turns a flaming red in autumn, plus cedars, pines and fir trees of every shape and form. ❦ Next came prairies, oceans of prairies, followed by the naked Rocky Mountains and Banff with its ghostly grand hotel stranded in the middle of the black forest surrounded by snowy peaks, sulphurous springs, waterfalls and raging torrents. Waiting to greet you in the entrance hall was a huge log fire flanked by firedogs with owls' heads. ❧ Hugging Fraser Canyon, the *Canadian Pacific* ran right along the bottom of the narrow gorge flowing with rushing water: the entire train seemed to float on the froth of the rapids that hurtled the tree trunks down to the sawmill. As it slipped through the log tunnels that protected the passengers from avalanches, they listened for sounds of snarling grizzlies. Look! There were Indians standing waist-high in water fishing for salmon. There were deer just visible among the teepees. Finally, the train reached Vancouver: a fiord, the mountains' unfathomable reflection, a delta hung with bridges, waters jumping with salmon

pursued by seals and the fishing boats of the insatiable canning factories. ❧ There was also a sea route linking North America's Atlantic coast with its Pacific coast which looped round the base of Central America. The ship hugged the "flowery" coast of Florida with its finger pointing to the Caribbean, its scattered reefs, and its "keys." The hotels on this coastline, from St. Augustine and Palm Beach to Miami, starting with the Alcazar and the Ponce de Leon, were all built of a local material called "coquina" made of shells and fossilized coral mixed with concrete. The entire coast is incrusted with sequins and paste, resembling an enormous diamanté slide in the flowery curls of the tropics. ❧ Then you reached Havana, "the key to the New World" as the Spaniards said and the city's coat-of-arms proclaimed. Next came the locks and ports of Colon, Cristobal and Balboa and the Panama Canal, that other great shortcut (after Suez) that lets us take a chunk out of the world map. You would have traveled back up the Californian coast to the Golden Gate that bars the entry to San Francisco. At that point it would have been hard to resist Honolulu with its elegant Waikiki Beach, especially the Moana Hotel with the sandalwood beams that had been in your dreams since the *S.S. Insulinde*. ❧ The seaside existence in Southern California, in San Diego, was like a transitional stage before Mexico, that "land of every excess." "In Mexico, there is no such thing as moderation" was the Indian's response to the English lady in D. H. Lawrence's *The Plumed Serpent*. The train would have traveled to Casas Grandes, one of America's oldest archaeological sites with its strange houses with 100 rooms on six floors that were half built into the side of the hillside. A brief shower on these dry cacti that were home to a few birds was enough to "make the desert bloom with multicolored flowers as mesquite bushes broke into pale yellow clusters, scapes of white bells sprouted from the rosettes of yuccas and garlands of red nipple cactus sparkled

among the stones." You would have passed through Monterrey, the free port of the lower Rio Grande valley with its magnificent gardens, and Mexico City the capital, then connected with a ship at Vera Cruz, the largest port in the country, surrounded by vanilla, sugar cane, coffee and tobacco. ❦ You then set off from the east coast of Mexico, steaming back through the Panama Canal, hugging the Pacific coast. Crossing the Equator was an excuse for endless practical jokes at the expense of more gullible souls, together with witty toasts of the type: "Sirs, let us raise our glasses to the beauty of the two hemispheres... and to the two hemispheres of beauty!" The ship put in at Mollendo where you

would have taken a Transandine train up the steepest railway in the world, passing first through Arequipa, an oasis at 7,600 ft and Peru's second major city, then Cuzco nestling in a magnificent valley at nearly 12,000 ft. The train went right to the top, to the roof of the world at 13,200 ft. The thrill of the giddy climb, however, was not the sole attraction of the journey: Cuzco, former capital of the Inca Empire whose name in Quechua means "umbilicus of the world" is a center of natural and man-made beauty, famous for its handcrafted woolen goods and jewelry. Further north lay the magical pre-Inca citadel of Machu Picchu that was missed by the Conquistadors and discovered by Hiram Bingham only in 1911. ❦ Returning to Mollendo, passengers set sail for Valparaíso, made famous by the French song *"Nous irons à*

Valparaiso." It was the second most important port in the Pacific after San Francisco and a welcome haven for sailors after the perils of Cape Horn. From there, another Transandine train traveled direct to Argentina and Buenos Aires, home of the celebrated tango where that leading exponent of tango music, Carlos Gardel, himself landed in 1893. Like so many Argentines, Gardel was of European descent, originally from Toulouse, France. The three-week crossing from Bordeaux, say, to South America ranked as long-haul travel compared to the Paris-New York shuttle. Three weeks was the time it took for the tango to reach Paris, where its sensuality caused a stir. "Is it danced standing up?" inquired the witty Countess Mélanie de Pourtalès. ❦ At the end of your world trip, you realized that you had not seen this, nor that either, not counting that you had promised yourself that you would… But the world was round. It had no beginning and no end and there was nothing to stop you from going round forever. So when would the next trip be?

Alain Rustenholz

Above: the Santa Fe to Mexico train with its bull bars in the 1870s. Poster for Banff Indian festivals in the period 1930-1940 (near right); guests on the terrace of the Royal Poinciana Hotel in Palm Beach in 1904 (far right).
Previous pages: two brochures for the *Compagnie Générale Transatlantique* (page 258) showing sailing times plus an invitation from the captain of the Paris to a couple of passengers, requesting the pleasure of their company at dinner and cocktails to welcome them aboard. Page 259: top, the Mexican steamship *Ypiranga* in the port of Vera Cruz and, bottom, a Cunard poster for the *Mauretania*, one of its most luxurious liners. Page 260: lunch menu for 27 February 1889 at the Ponce de Leon Hotel in St. Augustine, Florida. Page 261: top, family farewells before boarding the Chicago-to-San Francisco in 1889 and, bottom, Canadian Pacific poster c.1925 for the Royal York Hotel in Toronto, "the largest hotel in the British Empire." Insert page 257: cover of Pacific Line brochure, c. 1910.

EVERY MORNING SISLEY WOULD HAVE AN EARLY BREAKFAST OF TEA, toast and grapefruit on the terrace of the Château-Frontenac in Quebec, facing the St. Lawrence River and the Laurentian Mountains. Then he would light a Capstan and set out for his General Delivery mail.

Edouard Lavergne, 1941

The Château Frontenac in Quebec (1893) was one of a chain of new "château-style" hotels the Canadian Pacific Railway (C.P.R.) built along its route at the end of the 19th century. In *Palaces et Grands Hôtels d'Amérique du Nord*, Catherine Donzel tells the history of these "Citadels of the Trans-Canadian," the first of which was the Banff Springs Hotel (see pages 266-270). "For some it was characteristic of Germanic palatial architecture [whereas], for others it was a compromise between a Swiss chalet and a Tudor manor house," comments our author with a smile. Whatever the case, she continues, "château-style" was "an early manifestation of a theatrical, hybrid style that set out to seduce and impress [...]. For the Canadians [this approach] was for many decades the best expression of their national identity [...]: a style perfectly suited to a very young country that was in search of a past and cultural bearings." Above: time for refreshments at the edge of the ice rink in the 1940s. Right: the Dufferin Terrace adjoining the Château Frontenac and overlooking the St. Lawrence River, December 1988. Following double-page display: "equestrian" celebrations at the Frontenac in the 1950s. Pages 268-269: guests on a fine summer's day, c. 1930, on the banks of the Ottawa River in the grounds of the Château Montebello (C.P.R.'s other château-style hotel in Quebec).

THE TRUTH IS THAT PEOPLE IN THESE VAST COUNTRIES EVENTUALLY LOSE ALL SENSE OF DISTANCE. "You should go and se
Alaska," a Canadian friend was telling me in Seattle. "It's very close and very beautiful." "What do you call 'very close'"
I asked warily. "A week away," he answered in all innocence.

Maurice Rondet-Saint, 1923

The Banff Springs Hotel, built in 1888 in the heart of the Rockies, was designed by New York architect Bruce Price and commissioned by the C.P.R.'s Managing Director, W. C. Van Horne. "The breathtaking, dramatic beauty of the décor corresponded perfectly to the Wagnerian taste [of the period]," explains Catherine Donzel, who stayed at the Banff Springs. There were a few mistakes -- including building the panoramic rotunda at the rear of the hotel "that looked out onto the blank façade of Sulphur Mountain, whereas in the kitchens the staff enjoyed the extraordinary view of the Bow Valley ..." All the same, the hotel rapidly became a favorite with a European clientele accustomed to Swiss and Austrian resorts.

Above: golfers on the hotel green in the 1930s.

Right: the Banff and the Bow River (1920s) – the celebrated *River of No Return* in Otto Preminger's film shot on location in 1954 and starring Marilyn Monroe, who stayed at the hotel throughout the entire shoot. Following double-page display: left, tea at the Banff Springs in the summer of 1930 and, right, the same view of the river in the winter of 1988 with (almost) the same furnishings.

Insert: 1930s leaflet for the Château Lake Louise, the "chalet" of the Banff Springs Hotel.

IT WAS APPARENTLY ON A FINE SUMMER'S DAY IN 1882 that Tom Wilson discovered the immutable splendors of a lake well known to the Indians as the "Lake of the Little Fishes." It was subsequently renamed "Lake Louise" in homage to Princess Louise Caroline Alberta, Queen Victoria's daughter. Strangely this remarkable lake, that was exceptional as much for its position as for the color of its waters, never captured the C.P.R.'s commercial imagination …

Catherine Donzel, 1989

Château Lake Louise, just a few miles from Banff, was originally built as a simple wooden chalet for use by the many ramblers who went walking to Lake Louise. Faced with mounting numbers of visitors however, the C.P.R. converted it into a "château-style" hotel in 1913. Following a fire in 1924, it was replaced by a massive concrete building that did not fail to raise a few eyebrows. But view and traditions remain unchanged [however] and guests today can still gaze peacefully at the lake as they sip their hot chocolate, as they have done every winter since the Lake Louise first opened.
Above: a summer gathering by the lake in the 1930s.
Right: winter scene with workmen sweeping the snow from the frozen lake before the first skaters arrive.

I AM A CITY CHILD. I LIVE AT THE PLAZA. There is a lobby that is enormously large, with marble pillars and ladies in it and a revolving door with "P" on it.

Kay Thompson: Eloïse, 1948

shortly after it opened in 1907. When Simone de Beavoir first arrived in New York, she arranged by telephone to be at the Plaza Hotel on 59th Street at six o'clock. The overhead metro that she took to get there seemed more like a fairground ride with all the flickering lights and neon signs of the city beneath. Once there, she waited a long time in the hotel foyer – so long that she started to find it strange … "And suddenly I realized," she continues, "that I was in the Savoy-Plaza and that my meeting was across the street." Inset: Doorknob showing Plaza monogram with the two "P's" back-to-back referred to by Eloise, the heroine in the novel of the same name by Kay Thompson. The little girl lived in a suite at the Plaza Hotel and has become its mascot with her very own, specially designed and furnished "Eloise Suite" that is open to visitors.

Arriving in New York by sea was a slow process. If the ship had been delayed by thick fog, it would have been too late to sail up the river and you would have had to drop anchor in the bay until the following morning. The climate was so changeable that cloud could build up when the ship was maneuvering then suddenly be swept away by a gust of wind, revealing the most majestic dawn sky you had ever seen. Then, throwing a coat over your robe, you would have rushed to the rail to see the famous skyscrapers of the Manhattan skyline – at last!

Previous double-page display: passengers on the *Queen Mary* enjoying their first view of New York on 12 March 1939.
The Astor Hotel (above in 1909) "appeared to be crowned with lights. The balcony on the top floor [was] brilliantly lit, the sky was ablaze with the innumerable lights that were projected from the hanging gardens […]." (C. Donzel). The Astor and the "old" Waldorf-Astoria were once fierce rivals but the Astor had already been demolished when the new Waldorf-Astoria was built in 1929. Right: the celebrated Plaza Hotel

BROADWAY IS THE ARCHETYPAL MODEL OF THOSE MAJOR THOROUGHFARES linking the different parts of the continent, including both oceans [...] It is the major thoroughfare on the American mainland, a road more than a street, a royal road that stretches far and wide [...] The people visible in the countless vehicles are on their way to somewhere rather than passing through. They look worried rather than busy. It seems as though everyone has a train to catch.

Count Joseph von Hübner, 1886

Left: New York's Flatiron Building, built by Daniel H. Burnham in 1902 in the triangle formed by the crossing of Fifth Avenue and Broadway at 23rd Street, one block southwest of Madison Square Park. Rising 21 stories, it was the fourth skyscraper to emerge on the Manhattan skyline. Seen on the right is the same crossroads three years before the Flatiron Building was erected.
Previous double-page display: dinner at the Plaza in the early 1900s, the atmosphere bathed in the telltale Puritanism of New York at that time. Things had changed a bit since the days of the Wild West...

ALMOST ALL THE TRESS IN FLORIDA, especially the cedars and holm oaks, are covered from tip to toe with white moss [.
The multitude of butterflies, iridescent flies, humming birds, green budgerigars and blue jays that cling to the moss ma
it look like a white woolen tapestry that a European hand has embroidered with insects and brightly colored birds.
were resting in the shade of one of these charming natural refuges that are part of God's design. The great cedar sway
in the winds that blew down from the sky; the birds and the visitors asleep beneath its sheltering limbs floated off
the delicate castle founded on its branches and a thousand sighs seemed to emanate from the corridors and arches
this moving building. Never had the wonders of the Old World compared with this monument of the desert.

François René, Vicomte de Chateaubriand, 18

e coast of Florida boasts every
nceivable style of hotel, from the
ginal neo-Medieval style that
es from around 1885 – including
Alcazar and the Ponce de Leon
t were the work of Bernard
ybeck, architect of the Palace of
e Arts in San Francisco – to the
pano-Moorish style and the Art
co of the1930s. This astonishing
xture is made harmonious by
green palm trees, blue ocean
d golden sun.
ove: left, guests lunching
neath the trees in the gardens
he Royal Poinciana Hotel in
m Beach; right, the terrace of
npa Bay Hotel in Tampa City;
ow, the seaside promenade
ed with flowers leading to the
m Beach Hotel.
owing double-page display:

huge sandcastle built on the
beach of the Breakers Hotel in
Palm Beach in 1904. Insert: cover
of a special April 1926 issue of
the Literary Digest, featuring
vacations in Florida.
Previous double-page display: the
driver of the bus shown on page
283 had always dreamed of going
to Florida. One day, throwing
caution to the winds, he ordered
his passengers off the bus
(pictured here), sped past his
stops, ignored his terminus and
did not stop until he got there!
He became a national hero and,
of course, kept his job …which
just goes to show how seductive
Florida was. The bus of the Casa
Loma Hotel in Coral Gables,
shown on pages 284-5, enjoyed
no such notoriety.

Approach to Hotel Palm Beach, Palm Beach, Fla.

n FLORIDA

New Hollywood Hotel
On the Beach

GREAT SOUTHERN HOTEL

I TOOK A TAXI FROM RANCHO BOYEROS, THE AIRPORT, TO THE HOTEL TOLEDO [...] Shortly afterwards, clutching a glass o
cognac, I went out onto the terrace to look around. Next to the Toledo was another hotel, the El Vedada, where there wa:
a constant traffic of American tourists in loud, multicolored shirts. Further down was 23rd Street, the town's majo
thoroughfare and beyond that was the tall, solid, elegant building of the Hotel Nacional [...] The salty smell of the se:
wafted up to the place where I stood. I breathed in deeply and drained my glass

Jean Contenté, 1978

Havana c. 1920: three years of American administration were followed by a period of conditional independence. The picture on the left, taken recently, shows a convertible sports *coupé* tarnished by the tropical climate. It dates from the dark days of Prohibition when American tourists made a grateful beeline for Sloppy Joe's (above). When the USA lifted Prohibition in 1932, the managers of Havana's seedy bars and nightclubs turned to other markets. Mafia chief Meyer Lansky had no difficulty in obtaining permission from Fulgencio Battista – who had just taken power and was in dire financial straits – to open a casino in one of the city's

leading hotels, the Nacional. Within a short space of time the Mafia had created a flourishing industry and so began the "Belle Epoque of the Cuban casinos" that lasted until Fidel Castro took over. Following double-page display: Havana seen from a very different angle. The faded pink cathedral (almost) dates from the discovery of the New World. But these are all daytime images when what counts in these latitudes is night-time: real, genuine night-time, not the artificial pleasures spoken of above. "Those who have not seen the splendor of tropical nights cannot imagine the velvety pleasure of those hours spent beneath the veiled light of a

canopy of stars; they do not know the degree of ecstasy that can be felt by the physical body when bathed and caressed by this limpid atmosphere; it engages all the senses and every movement is such a pleasure that it is as if weight were no longer a restriction" wrote (would you believe it!) the very austere geographer Elisée Reclus in 1885.

CUBA

WHO HAS FORGOTTEN the wave of horror that swept the entire universe at the news that San Francisco had been wiped out — the place that Yankees call "'Frisco"? [...] In fact, it has not yet been rebuilt and offers a spectacle of the most astonishing contrast. All the big companies and millionaires have rebuilt their skyscrapers or "buildings" as they say in the States [...] Others are in course of completion. Next to them [...] stand yesterday's buildings in ruins. [...] In the midst of all this loom huge, brand-new luxury hotels [...] On the hill overlooking the city towers the majestic outline of a hotel that is often depicted in engravings over here: the Fairmont Palace...

Maurice Rondet-Saint, 1924

CALIFORNIA

Simone de Beauvoir first caught sight of San Francisco from the end of the Golden Gate Bridge when she was driving along the coastal route at a tangent to the city. But she saw it as she was driving away from it! She wanted to stop, turn around but both were out of the question on the toll bridge. The "Golden Gate" was closed to her. In those days, it was truer to its name than it is today: copper-colored with a gilded hue that had been chosen by popular vote. Market Street (right), a long, almost level avenue in an otherwise hilly town, runs from the ferry landing stage through the Mission District with its Latin-American population toward Twin Peaks.
Left: the Coronado Hotel opened in 1888 in San Diego Bay. To the north was a Naval Air Command base, to the south was the submarine base that proved a valuable source of military guests. This is where Charles Lindbergh's *Spirit of St. Louis* was built and Thomas Edison himself installed

the hotel's electricity — even returning at Christmas time to decorate the tree with fairy lights. The history of the Coronado reads like an immense book of records. Guests include the Prince of Wales and 12 Presidents of the United States, and the hotel itself was the setting for Billy Wilder's *Some Like It Hot*. It was classified as a historic monument in 1977. The immense pointed tower that now symbolizes the hotel once served as a water tower; all of its 400 bedrooms — currently 700 — gave onto the raised pathways of a magnificent interior garden.

HE SAW THE BEARS IN YELLOWSTONE PARK, the giant sequoias, the orange groves and the oil wells, the patios in Santa Barbara, the old Spanish missions and the Mexicans of Imperial Valley. He went fishing for abalone on small islands inhabited by thousands of seals. He went all the way to San Diego to visit the American squadron in the Pacific and lingered over the finest Lawrence and Gainsborough canvases in the Huntington Art Gallery.

Edouard Lavergne, 1941

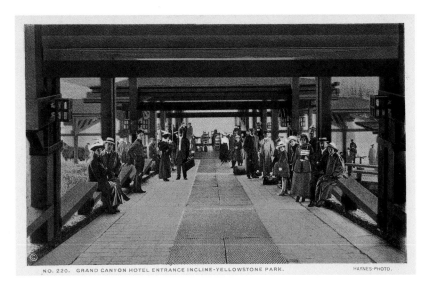

NO. 220. GRAND CANYON HOTEL ENTRANCE INCLINE-YELLOWSTONE PARK.   HAYNES-PHOTO.

Above, c. 1900, is the ramp leading down to the Grand Canyon Hotel that clings to the rock face in Yellowstone National Park in the heart of the Rocky Mountains. Created in 1872 and reached by a small railway that connected with the Northern Pacific, Yellowstone Park is a volcanic region where geysers cover the mountainous vegetation with astonishing incrustations and subterranean rivers alternate with sheer canyons.

Right: the spectacular Ahwahnee Hotel that opened in the heart of Yosemite National Park on 14 July 1927. It took a team of 245 people 18 months to build it. Yosemite Park is 188 miles east of San Francisco and covers an area of nearly 1,875 sq. miles. In 1905 Yosemite was returned to federal control; it includes some of the most famous sites in the USA including Lake Mirror, the Bridal Veil Falls with the Virgin's Tears opposite, and the *El Capitan* Rock.

MEXICO [...] HAD JUST TAKEN A DECISIVE STEP FORWARD [...] with the completion of the Trans-Pacific Mexican Railway from Vera Cruz to Mazanillo via Mexico City and Guadalajara. The line had been solemnly inaugurated barely two months before our arrival. [...] We therefore had a rare opportunity to see a new country that just yesterday was practically inaccessible, from the comfort of our balcony platform. [...] The train stopped at interminable stations but this was an added attraction because of the delightful crowds who rushed to see a sight they had never seen before: people dressed in fashionable city clothes or colonial uniforms complete with pith helmets that seemed especially amusing. The ladies in particular [...] were a great success. Nor did we ever seem to tire of the unusual nature of these people.

Maurice Rondet-Saint, 1924

Calle de Gante, City of Mexico.
Sonora News Company, City of Mexico

In the autumn of 1936, the Hotel Reforma de Mexico commissioned Diego Rivera to design four frescoes with a carnival theme plus a series of nude pin-ups for its bar, Ciro's. The models were young girls of excellent family who were delighted to be thus immortalized in art. Works by the Marxist muralist were a tourist attraction in these parts. In January 1937, Trotsky sought refuge in Mexico and was welcomed to Tampico by Frida Kahlo on behalf of Diego Rivera, who was sick. They traveled by presidential train, the *Hidalgo*, to Coyoacan, a suburb of the capital, where Frida offered Trotsky the run of "a low-built, blue house with a patio full of plants, cool rooms, collections of pre-Colombian art, a multitude of paintings ..." The Reforma's frescoes were removed before the hotel was inaugurated (Rivera had taken the wise precaution of making them portable after John D. Rockefeller, Jr. ordered him to destroy the one that he had commissioned for Rockefeller Center in New York). Photographer André Breton made a visit to Mexico in the Spring of 1938 and expressed his enthusiasm for this "land of convulsive beauty," "this surrealist place par excellence." Above: a street in Mexico City, the Calle de Gante, c. 1900. Right: the colonnaded balcony overlooking the lush garden of the appropriately named "Hotel Garden" in Mexico City in the 1930s. Following double-page display: the hotel staff pose for a "souvenir photograph" in the former lobby of the Hotel Geneva in Mexico City, now the Jardin Restaurant of the Hotel Calinda Geneva.

E X I C O

I. K. 12, México.   *Hôtel Iturbide. México.*

Left: the glass roof designed by Jacques Gruber (of the Ecole de Nancy) and the elevator of the Gran Hotel Ciudad de Mexico. The interior of this late 19th-century building that originally served as a shopping center was entirely refurbished in Art Nouveau style around 1908. It was only converted to a hotel in recent years.

Right: the baroque Italian-style palace that was home to Agostin Iturbide, army commander in Mexico's successful War of Independence against Spain in 1821.

Following double-page display: the construction of the Inca citadels was a Herculean task. It involved the precise positioning of polygonal – not rectangular – blocks of stone, some weighing nearly 20 tons, that held together solely by compression – the Incas used no mortar. Machu Picchu was the last bastion of Manco Inca's resistance against the Spanish Pizarro brothers. Having successfully thwarted 300 years of relentless exploration, it was finally discovered in 1911 by Hiram Bingham, a Senator in the U.S. Congress. This steeply terraced Inca city, famous for its elliptically shaped Temple of the Sun and its plain, unadorned buildings, rises to the top of the mountain. There, on fields the size of postage stamps, the Incas cultivated a cereal called "quinoa" that grows at high altitudes, plus a wider selection of vegetables than any other civilization in the world. These dizzy heights are the natural habitat of the vicuña, a species of *Camelidae* that is impossible to domesticate but can be caught just long enough to shear. Vicuña have a nasty habit of spitting in your face.

IT WAS STILL NIGHT WHEN, THE FOLLOWING DAY AND WITHIN THE HOTEL COURTYARD ITSELF, we settled into the comfortable carriages of our Transandine train. The track clung nervously to the mountainside in an immense corrie, passing through short tunnels and continuing upward to 10,000 ft where there is a basin formed by mountains more than 20,000 ft high that slope down to a lake [...]. It is known as the Inca Lake because, according to legend, somewhere round here lies the Inca gold that Pizarro never managed to find.

Maurice Rondet-Saint, 1924

Left, the Valparaiso Stock
Exchange c. 1900. In 1535, Diego
de Almagro and his men left
Cuzco to explore the South as far
as the Straits of Magellan. They
never reached the Straits but the
natural port that they discovered
on the way was so beautiful that
they called it Valparaiso (Valley of
Paradise). On a more mundane
level, it became the railhead of the
Transandine Railway (above).
Completed in 1910, the line was
the southernmost link between the
South Pacific and South Atlantic
oceans. Europeans traveling to
Chile by the northern sea route via
Panama or the southern route

round the Straits of Magellan
could now clip a few days off their
journey. From Buenos Aires the
train set out across the pampas,
then along the first of the Andean
terraces to the Cordilleras and the
Cumbre Pass at 12,300 ft. At these
altitudes, trains needed the type of
snowplow seen above.
Following double-page display: the
first pilgrimage on 22 February
1908 to the international
monument of Christ of the Andes,
symbol of peace between
Argentina and Peru.

The abiding image of Argentina for me will always be of a large hide stretched out to dry in the sun. I picture a capital beneath a magnificent winter sky where everything is edible: tender fleshed houses, roads made of muscle, hearts of filet, boneless cutlets with no gristle ... Buenos Aires, at the mouth of the Plate Estuary, on the banks of the 50-mile wide River Rio, with its gray-blue, mother-of-pearl lagoon, its silver beach shimmering beneath pockets of blue sky and its narrow channel marked out with black buoys.

Paul Morand, 1932

In Buenos Aires, the boardwalk (left) seems as long as the interminable pampas, those grassy plains that start as you leave Rio and extend along the right-bank of the Plate to cover an area more than six times the size of California. From that vast ocean of flatness relieved only by the domes of Congress Square, come taciturn *gauchos*, cowboys who occasionally gallop into town for a cup of hot *maté* served in a scooped-out gourd and who, after dancing in silence for a while, leave as quickly as they arrive. Right: memories of the capital of Argentina, c. 1920, as captured in photographs of the period and a photograph album.
Following double-page display: onlookers wave goodbye as the *Orontes* sets out off for Australia. On board is the English cricket team bound for their world tour of 1932.

Buenos Aires

Bibliography

Andreas-Salomé, Lou, *En Russie avec Rilke*, 1900, Seuil, 1992

Baudelaire, "Anywhere out of the world," and "L'Invitation au voyage," *Le Spleen de Paris*, Collected Works, Gallimard, 1961

Baudelaire, "L'Invitation au voyage," "Le Voyage," dedicated to Maxime du Camp, 1859, *Les Fleurs du Mal*, Collected Works, Gallimard, 1961

Beauvoir, Simone (de) *La force de l'Age*, Gallimard, 1960; *La Force des Choses*, Gallimard, 1963; *L'Amérique au Jour le Jour*, Gallimard, 1954

Berchet, Jean-Claude, *Le Voyage en Orient*, Collection Bouquins, Robert Laffont, 1985

Bernand, Carmen and **Gruzinski**, Serge, *Histoire du Nouveau Monde*, Fayard, 1991

Boissier, Raymond, *Dans Marrakech, la Rouge*, in "Marrakech Années 20," Ommès et Co., 1930,

Boissieu, Jean, *Quand Marseille Tenait les Clés de l'Orient*, Fayard, 1982

Bonnetain, Paul, *L'Extrême-Orient*, Maison Quantin, Paris, 1887

Bowles, Paul, based on *Let it Come Down*, London, John Lehmann, 1952

Brauquier, Louis, *Le Bar d'Escale*, Aix-en-Provence, "Le Feu," 1926

Brautigan, Richard, *Un Privé à Babylone*, Bourgois, 1981

Broué, Pierre, *Trotsky*, Fayard, 1988

Butor, Michel, *La Modification*, Minuit, 1957

C. & R. L., based on *Notes by the Way Round the Wide World*, Glasgow, David Hobbes & Co, 1900

Camus, Albert, *Noces*, "L'été à Ager," Gallimard, 1959

Célarié, Henriette, *Un Mois au Maroc*, Hachette, 1923

Cendrars, Blaise, *Moravagine*, Grasset, 1926

Cendrars, Blaise, *La Prose du Transsibérien et de la Petite Jehanne de France*, Gallimard, 1913

Chateaubriand, François René, Vicomte de, *Atala*,1801 and *Les Voyages en Amérique et en Italie*, 1827

Chevrillon, André, *Marrakech dans les Palmes*, Calmann-Lévy, 1919

Christie, Agatha, based on *Murder on the Orient-Express*, Collins, 1934

Christie, Agatha, based on *The Mystery of the Blue Train*, Collins, 1972

Christie, Agatha, based on *Murder in Mesopotamia*, Collins, 1936

Christie, Agatha, *Death on the Nile*, HarperCollins, 1956

Cohen, Albert, *Belle du Seigneur*, Gallimard, 1968

Contenté, Jean, *L'Aigle des Caraïbes*, Laffont, 1978

Cortambert, Richard, *Voyage Pittoresque à Travers le Monde*, Librairie Hachette, 1884

Cunard, Nancy, *Grand Man: Memories of Norman Douglas*, Secker and Warburg, 1954

Delvaille, Bernard, *Et l'au-delà de Suez*, André Dimanche, 1987

Dethier, Jean, Delacroix, Paul, *Gares d'Europe*, Denoël, 1984

Donleavy, J.P., based on *The Saddest Summer of Samuel S*, Eyre & Spottiswood, 1967

Donzel, Catherine, "Les Citadelles du Transcanadien," in *Grands Hôtels d'Amérique*, Flammarion, 1989

Dorgelès, Roland, *Partir...*, Albin Michel, 1926

Dostoevsky, *The Gambler*, based on an original 1915 translation by C.J. Hogarth, revised for Everyman in 1994.

Duras, Marguerite, *Le Vice-Consul*, Gallimard, 1966

Eberhardt, Isabelle, *Notes de Route*, Actes Sud, 1998

Fitzgerald, Scott, *Tender is the Night*, Everyman, 1996

Gaillard, André, in Bernard Delvaille, *Et l'au-delà de Suez*, André Dimanche, 1987

Garro, Frédérique, **Lapouge**, Gilles, *Notes sur l'Inde*, in "Traverses 41/42," Éditions du Centre Pompidou, 1987

Grève, Claude (de), *Le Voyage en Russie*, Collection Bouquins, Laffont, 1990

Hersant, Yves, *Italies*, Collection Bouquins, Laffont, 1988

Hilton, Conrad, based on *Be My Guest*, Prentice-Hall, Inc., New Jersey, 1957.

Hübner, Joseph Alexander, Count von, *À travers l'Empire Britannique*, Librairie Hachette, 1886

Jackson, Stanley, based on *The Savoy, the Romance of a Great Hotel*, F. Miller, Ltd,

Kyria, Pierre, *Jean Lorrain*, Seghers, 1973

Lagrillière-Beauclerc, F., *Voyages Pittoresques à Travers le Monde*, Coll. Ch. Taillandier, 1900

Larbaud, Valéry, Ode; *Schveningue, Morte-Saison*; Thalassa; Images; Europe; *L'ancienne Gare de Cahors*, in "Les Poésies de A. O. Barnabooth," Gallimard, 1948

Larbaud, Valéry, *A.O. Barnabooth, Son Journal Intime*, Gallimard, 1913

Lavergne, Édouard, *Les Voyageurs Chimériques*, Lardanchet, 1941

Leadbeater, C. W., Based on a translation from the French of "Le Lotus Bleu,"1929-1930, in *Extrême-Orient*, Agenda Adyar, 1932. Original source not available.

Leroux, Gaston, *Œuvres*, Collection Bouquins, Robert Laffont, 1984

La Chine, des Pays et des Hommes, collective work, Librarie Larousse, 1983

Londres, Albert, *Marseille, Porte du Sud*, L.E.F., 1927

Londres, Albert, *Mourir pour Changhaï*, 1932 UGE, 1984

Lorrain, Jean, *Heures d'Afrique*, 1899, Charpentier 1930

Loti, Pierre, *Voyages (1872-1913)*, Collection Bouquins, Laffont, 1991

Lowry, Malcolm, based on *Under the Volcano*, Cape, 1947

Malraux, André, *Antimémoires*, Gallimard 1967

Manifeste du Futurisme, Milan, le 11 avril 1910

Mann, Paul, *Season of the Monsoon*, Fawcett Crest, 1992

Mann, Thomas, *Pariser Rechenschaften*, in "L'Artiste et la société: portraits, études, souvenirs," Grasset 1973.

Mann, Thomas, *Death in Venice*, in Death in Venice and Other Stories, translated by David Luke, Minerva 1996

Méry, Joseph, *Marseille et les Marseillais*, Librairie Nouvelle, 1860

Morand, Paul, *Air Indien*, Grasset, 1932

Morand, Paul, *Flèche d'Orient*, N.R.F., 1932

Morand, Paul, *Ouvert la Nuit*, N.R.F., 1922

Mouhot, Henri, *Voyages dans les Royaumes de Siam, de Laos, de Cambodge et d'Autres Parties Centrales de l'Indochine*, 1864

Mousset, Paul, *Le Chemin de l'Extrême Orient*, Del Duca, 1956

Nizan, Paul, *Intellectuel Communiste*, Maspero, 1970

Palaces d'Europe, by a group of authors, Flammarion, 1984

Palaces d'Orient, by a group of authors, Flammarion, 1987

Paris/Berlin, Centre Georges Pompidou, 1978

Parrot, Louis, *Paul Eluard*, Seghers, 1964

Reclus, Elisée, quoted by Henriette Chardak, *Elisée Reclus, L'Homme qui Aimait la Terre*, Stock, 1997

Rilke, letters to Lou Andréas-Salomé, in *Correspondance*, Gallimard, 1980-1985

Rilke, Rainer-Maria, *Lettres Françaises à Merline*, Seuil, 1950

Rondet-Saint, Maurice, *La Grande Boucle*, Librairie Plon, 1924

Schnitzler, Arthur, *Lettres aux Amis 1886-1901*, Rivages, 1991

Senneville, Gérard (de), *Maxime du Camp*, Stock, 1996

Shenker, Israel, *The Savoy of London*, The Savoy and Chesler Publications, 1988

Temime, Emile, *Histoire de Marseille de la Révolution à Nos Jours*, Perrin, 1999

Tharaud, Jérôme and Jean, *Marrakech ou les Seigneurs de l'Atlas*, Plon 1920, in Berthaud Michel, Marrakech Années 20, "L Croisée des Chemins," 1997

Thompson, Kay, *Eloise*; Simon & Schuster Books for Young Readers, 1983

Tours, Constant (de), *La Belgique* May et Motteroz, Paris, 1895

Verne, Jules, *Les Enfants du Capitaine Grant*, Voyage Autour d Monde, J. Hetzel, 1867-68

Verne, Jules, *Le Tour du monde e Quatre-Vingts Jours*, J. Hetzel, 187

Weiss, Louise, *Mémoires d'une Européenne*, TII 1919-34, and TIII 1934-39, Albin Michel, 1980

Yon, Jean-Claude, *Jacques Offenbach*, Gallimard, 2000

Zweig, Stefan, *La Confusion des Sentiments*, Stock, 1929

Zweig, Stefan, *Le Joueur d'Echecs*, Delachaux et Niestlé, 1972

Zweig, Stefan, *Vingt-Quatre heures de la Vie d'Une Femme*, Stock, 1981

‍able of Quotations

Photographic credits

Jacques Boulay: 74-75 ; C.P.R : 227, 261 bottom, 262, 264, 266/67, 268/69, 270, 271, 272, 274; Jean-Noël de Soye: 45 ; Catherine Donzel: 265, 273, 275; all rights reserved: 171, 181, 202, 210; Éric d'Hérouville/l'Art de voyager: 4, 187, 188, 189; Hulton Getty Picture Collection: 164, 276/77, 312/13; Guillaume de Laubier: 58/59, 95, 98/99; Patrick Lébédeff: 1, 203, 218 to 221; André Martin: 304/05; Patrimoine Photographique © French Ministry of Culture: 16 (photo: Marcel Bovis), 101 (photo: Daniel Boudinet); Photothèque Hachette: 13, 22, 104, 105, 106/07, 108 (Vérascopes Richard), 124, 125, 134, 135, 168 (above), 177 (Vérascopes Richard), 194/95, 225 (above), 234 (above), 236/37, 239 (Vérascopes Richard), 240/41, 292/93, 295, 306 and 307 (Vérascopes Richard), 308/309; Robert Polidori: 280; Raffles Hotel Heritage Collection: 214; Scope: 2/3 and 146 (Charles Bowman), 204/05 (Michel Gotin); Anil Sharma: 6, 11, 167, 182/83, 184/85, 300/01, 302 Archives Vuitton: 9; Collection Walter : 10, 12, 17, 18, 20, 21, 24/25, 30/31, 32, 33, 36, 38 to 39, 40 and 41 (photo C. Hielscher), 42 to 45, 48 to 57, 60 to 73, 76 to 80, 82 to 86, 90 to 94, 100, 102/03, 109 to 115, 119, 120, 121, 122, 126 to 129, 147 to 161, 163, 168 (bottom), 169, 170, 172 à 176, 178/79, 180, 186, 197, 198/99, 200, 206, 211, 216/17, 225 (bottom), 226, 238, 242 et 243 (photo H. van Perckhammer), 244 to 249, 252 to 255, 259, 260, 261, 262, 263, 278/79, 280/81, 282/83, 284/85, 286, 287, 288/89, 294, 296, 297, 298, 299, 303, 310 ; photos Marc Walter: 8, 19, 23, 26, 27, 28/29, 34/35, 37, 46/47, 81, 87, 88/89, 118, 123, 130/31, 132/33, 136/37, 138/39, 140 to 145, 162, 190 to 193, 196, 201, 207, 208/09, 212/13, 215, 224, 228 to 233, 235, 250/51, 258, 281, 311.

Acknowledgments

This book would not have been possible without the help and advice of certain people, especially those who have provided us with information that we could not have obtained otherwise. Our thanks in particular to Catherine Donzel for her invaluable information on the grand hotels of the Orient and America and for her photographs of Canada. Our warmest thanks also to Patrick Lébédeff for his friendly and generous contribution, to Colette Véron for her enthusiasm, advice and support and to Nancy Dorking who trusted us with her great aunt's valise.
Alain Rustenholz wishes to express his personal thanks to Babette Leforestier who provided him with "Notes by the way," the diary of a journey made by an English preacher and his wife who traveled from Bath on 7 June 1899 on an evangelistic world tour. We are grateful to Gretchen Liu and the Raffles Hotel archives, to Sylvain Calvier, M. Zisul, Isabelle David, editor in chief of the magazine "L'Art de Voyager," to Sylvie Gabriel, head of the Hachette Photo Library and to Yann Martin who sent us a photograph by André Martin. Our thanks also to the following photographers: Jacques Boulay, Guillaume de Laubier, Eric d'Hérouville, Robert Polidori, Jean-Noël de Soye and Anil Sharma.
Finally we would like to thank Florence Cailly and Emilie Greenberg.

First published in France in 2001 by Editions du Chêne - Hachette-Livre
Copyright © 2001 Editions du Chêne — Hachette-Livre

This edition published by the Michael Friedman Publishing Group, Inc.
by arrangement with Editions du Chêne — Hachette-Livre

ISBN: 1-58663-718-5
2002 Friedman/Fairfax
1 3 5 7 9 10 8 6 4 2
For bulk purchases and special sales, please contact:
Michael Friedman Publishing Group, Inc.
Attention: Sales Department
230 Fifth Avenue, Suite 700
New York, NY 10001
212/685-6610 FAX 212/685-3916
Visit our website: www.metrobooks.com